DESPERATE PRAYERS FOR DESPERATE SITUATIONS

DESPERATE PRAYERS FOR DESPERATE SITUATIONS

Unleashing God's Power in the Dead Ends of Life

ALFRED 'BISI TOFADE

FOREWORD DR. CINDY TRIMM

QUICK READ BOOK SERIES

ACKNOWLEDGEMENTS

This book is dedicated to the honor and glory of the Most High, who rules in the affairs of men.

I also dedicate it to my lovely wife, Toyin, for all the prayers and support over the years, and to our sons, Christopher Olaoluwa and David Oladeji. You are all my joy and inspiration.

I wish to acknowledge my congregation, Jubilee Christian Church International, Chapel of Victory, and all the servants of God here in North Carolina, the entire Jubilee family in the United States.

Special thanks to Dr. Cindy Trimm, a great and inspiring leader, speaker, and writer for her time and valuable suggestions on this book. I wish to show special appreciation to Ms Ebun Odeneye and Ms Adwoa Akwabi-Ameyaw for reviewing the initial manuscript and adding great ideas. May the Lord bless you richly.

CONTENTS

Foreword ix
Introduction: Desperate situations of life xiii

1. Prayer Moves the Hands of God 17
2. Blind Bartimaeus: *This is it or never!* 29
3. The Pleadings of Hannah: *Pushing through the barriers* . . . 41
4. Desperate Hezekiah: The prayer of a dying man: *"Lord, I am not ready!"* 57
5. Elijah on Mount Carmel: *Releasing what is promised* 67
6. The Struggle of Jacob: *"I will not let you go until..."* 77
7. Let Go, Let God! 87

Conclusion: *100 Prayer Points for Different Desperate Situations* 95
Bibliography 103

Dr. Cindy Trimm

FOREWORD

To rephrase the statement made by Eugene Peterson when making comments about the book of Psalms in the writing of *The Message Bible* published by NavPress, the Jews, with several centuries of a head start on us in matters of prayers and devotions to God used the book of Psalms to construct their prayers and engineer their worship. Several writers, which included king David, Moses and King Solomon, all acquainted with the full range of human emotions, provided them with a language adequate for responding to the God who created the heavens and earth and to entreat him in times of need. This is exactly what Dr. Bisi Tofade has attempted to do with this book entitled, *"Desperate Prayers For Desperate Situations"* – to give the reader a go-to-reference book in the times of their greatest need.

As a preacher of the gospel, I was charged with, the wonderful assignment to teach people to pray; helping them to give voice to their emotions and human experiences as they navigated their spiritual walk with God. The impulse to pray is deep within us all and in its simplest form flows naturally from the core of our being. "Dear God", "Bless my children", bless my home", "and bless this meal" and "...In Jesus Name!" is our basic prayers. In desperation we exclaim, "Oh God" or

"Jesus". But developing the vocabulary, stamina and consistency is yet another task which doesn't come quite as spontaneously and easily. We must be coached.

Faced with the prospect of conversing with a holy God, the disciples asked Jesus to teach them to pray. He gave them a simple formula that was based on their relationship with God as their heavenly Father. Dr. Tofade's book on prayer is a book that is built upon this simple truth, that our heavenly Father loves us and wants the best for us all. He wants to bless us beyond our wildest imagination. This is the basis for our prayers. We can go to Him and expect a favorable response to all of our prayers. Desperate times call for desperate measures. Prayer is exactly that. And as we cry out to God, according to Hebrews 4:16, "we will find grace to help in time of need."

Just like anything else, when we first begin praying, there is a tendency to feel awkward, especially when our prayers are desperate. What do you say? How do you address God during times of disappointment, sadness, hurt and pain? What about discussing your shortcomings and mistakes with God? Have you thought of that? Most people believe that they need to be perfect before they can approach God. But they don't. God hears the prayers of everyone. You don't have to feel that you are not good enough, or smart enough or talented enough or articulate enough or spiritual enough to pray. You no longer have to feel as if you have to wait until you clean up your act or prove that you are qualified.   Your prayers do not have to be polished or polite, grammatically correct or eloquent when you are desperate. Let your passion drive you to your place of power, healing, forgiveness and peace – that's what prayer is all about. When you read this book it will help to dispel faulty ideas concerning God's willingness to answer your prayers.

Recently I re-read the book of psalms. The language is not always polished and polite, because many of the psalms were prayed from the lips of a desperate person. Ignorantly, we tend to think that praying is what good people do when they are doing their best. It is not. Inexperienced, we suppose that there must be a "special" language that must be learned before God takes notice of our prayers. There is not. Prayer is the simplest way to express the wide variety of experiences

you are having while trying to make sense out of life. It is the means by which you can talk to God honestly, truthful, and in response to the promises made to us all in James 5:16 "The effectual fervent prayer of a righteous man availeth much." When you pray desperate prayers, you will get incredible results and find gratifying results.

Dr. N. Cindy Trimm, #1 Bestselling Author of *The Art of War For Spiritual Battles*, *The Rules of Engagement* and *Commanding Your Morning*
www.Trimminternational.com

DESPERATE SITUATIONS OF LIFE

MATTHEW 11:12
And from the days of John the Baptist until now the kingdom
of heaven suffereth violence, and the violent take it by force.

It was a desperate moment that morning in the hall. There was no
supply left and the staff was anxious about what to give the children
for breakfast. There were hundreds of mouths to feed, children who
had no clue there was no bread and milk for breakfast. George, the
director of the orphanage, was informed immediately. He had something about him, an aura of peace and confidence in God. He ordered
the children to sit in the hall while he led prayer over the empty cups.
He knew God would come through in the nick of time.

He had barely finished praying when suddenly there was a knock.
It was the baker. "Mr. Mueller," he said, "I couldn't sleep last night.
Somehow I felt you didn't have bread for breakfast, so I got up at 2
a.m. and baked some fresh bread." A second knock sounded. The
milkman's truck had broken down right in front of the orphanage,
and he wanted to give the children his milk so he could empty his
wagon and repair it.

God had come through in a desperate situation for His servant, even if He had to give the baker insomnia and the milkman a flat tire.

Have you ever been in a situation where you know unless God intervenes, nothing else will work? Are you facing what I refer to as the "deadly three": disappointment, discouragement, and defeat, and all hope that things will turn around is gone?

There are times and situations in life when things are tough and challenging; sometimes it appears we are at the end of the rope or at an intersection that reads "dead end." These are days that I refer to as desperate days. It may be a financial situation, a family crisis, a deadline to meet or beat, or a situation getting out of hand. Many are facing personal defeats or nervous breakdowns, and some have even committed suicide because they were so overwhelmed.

In times like these, our ticket to victory is to engage in desperate prayers.

Many have been there before and they sank into it, others simply gave up and surrendered to defeat, but I want to offer you what you need to rise above the situation—tough faith and purpose-driven prayer.

The devil will always be evil; his job is to attack you, your health, your dreams, your marriage, your finances, etc. It could be strange to live a life free of attacks. None of us should be surprised when we face opposition, fear, and challenges. We officially declared ourselves to be Satan's enemy the day we accepted Christ, and he has formally accepted our invitation as his adversaries. However, we need not fear defeat when the Lord is on our side.

Let us review the scriptural reference again:

"From the days...till now...." Desperate days. "...the kingdom... suffers violence," a special assault from the gate of hell against the destiny of men. The demons were desperate to stop men, hold down their destiny, and destroy their joy.

Yes, many were victimized and brutalized; many were trampled down, the inheritance of the weak ones were vandalized by these desperate and determined cohorts of hell.

But wait, there were a few who stood their ground and resisted the enemy. They took what was theirs by force. How? By determined and desperate prayers!

Prayer changes things, yet many don't have time for it. As you read through this book, I want you to seize the opportunity of powerful prayers of saints seen in the Bible to change some ugly things in your life. Jacob prayed until his name was changed (Genesis 32:24–32). Jabez prayed desperately until the curse was broken (1 Chronicles 4:9–10). Hezekiah prayed until his lifespan was extended (2 Kings 20:1–11).

From the great testimonies of many lives in the Scriptures, I wish to draw examples of lives that were transformed through the power of prayer poured from their desperate souls to God in their desperate days.

These were not ordinary prayers and petitions; they were uttered in difficult and tough circumstances. They received tremendous answers from God. We are dealing with the same God today. He is no respecter of persons.

DESPERATE DAYS IN OUR LIVES

When You Need Desperate Prayers

You need desperate prayers when there are problems and troubles staring at you right in the face that you cannot ignore, dismiss, or avoid. Problems in your path wherever you go, yelling at you, "I am still here, like your shadow, and there is nothing you can do about me."

When you have a stubborn problem that is resisting remedy, only **stubborn faith** and **stubborn persistence** will uproot it. Have you experienced a stubborn situation lately? Activate your faith and be persistent in prayers to handle these types of situations.

Chapter 1

PRAYER MOVES THE HANDS OF GOD

WHAT IS A DESPERATE MOMENT?

There is a story in the book of Acts Chapter 12. It was a time of severe persecution for the Church. One of the Apostles called James was arrested and executed by Herod the king. Soon after, he got Peter arrested too and was planning the same fate for him.

The church fearing for the life of Peter began to engage heaven in prayer on his behalf. It was a difficult night, Peter; bound among soldiers in a heavily guarded prison was scheduled to be killed in the morning. It was amazing that Peter slept soundly. He knew his life was in the hands of God. Believers gathered in the house of one the disciples and prayed earnestly for God to intervene in the situation.

Suddenly, an angel appeared, walked through the iron doors, went pass the guards, unloosed Peter's chain and stole him out of the place. What a miracle, what an intervention in a desperate moment!

- When you are dealing with disappointments of life such as broken relationships or unfulfilled expectations (like John in Matthew 11:2–3)
- When you are being pursued by problems that threaten to swallow you (like Elijah in 1 Kings 19:4)
- When you are facing a delay in getting answers to your prayers, yet there is no sin in your life
- When you are experiencing a time of great loss in your family or business and sufferings and misfortunes

Prayer is conversing with God; it is the intercourse of the soul with God in direct address to Him. It is "beseeching the LORD" (Exodus 32:11); "pouring out the soul before the LORD" (1 Samuel 1:15); "praying and crying to heaven" (2 Chronicles 32:20); "seeking unto God and making supplication" (Job 8:5); "drawing near to God" (Psalm 73:28); and "bowing the knees" (Ephesians 3:14).

- *A man of prayer can touch heaven. The tallest man on earth is the one on his knees.*
- *"I fear the prayer of John Knox more than the army of England."* –Queen Mary
- *Faith can move mountains; the prayer of saints can move the hands that control the universe to act.*

- *Prayer closed the mouth of lions; prayer opened the prison doors, and Peter walked away a free man (Acts 12).*
- *Prayer stopped the movement of the sun and the moon (Joshua 10:12).*
- *Prayer sealed the heavens, brought down fire from heaven, and brought down rain.*

JAMES 5:16–18

Confess your faults one to another, and pray one for another, that ye may be healed. The effectual fervent prayer of a righteous man availeth much.

Elias was a man subject to like passions as we are, and he prayed earnestly that it might not rain: and it rained not on the earth by the space of three years and six months.

And he prayed again, and the heaven gave rain, and the earth brought forth her fruit.

Prayer can cross any barrier—including the oceans and continents of the world. It travels faster than the speed of light. It affects the present and controls the future. Prayer is invisible, yet it is very potent.

> ## Whatever prayer cannot do is what God cannot... and there is nothing!

INGREDIENTS OF A PRAYER THAT AVAILS MUCH

Prayer is like an arrow that has a specific target when shot. For the arrowhead to be effective and not miss its intended target, certain principles must be engaged to guide it. This is what is referred to as effective praying.

For result-producing prayers, the following are vital:
- Prayer must be offered in the name of Jesus (Acts 4:12).
- Prayer must be according to the will of God (Romans 8:27; Matthew 26:39).

- Prayer must be specific and result-oriented. Don't pray for praying's sake (James 5:16).
- Prayer must be done in faith (Hebrews 11:6; Mark 11:23).
- Prayer must be made in the context of intimacy with God.

Consider these examples:

i. Prayer of Moses, a servant of God

Exodus 33:11–18

And the Lord spake unto Moses face to face, as a man speaketh unto his friend. And he turned again into the camp: but his servant Joshua, the son of Nun, a young man, departed not out of the tabernacle.

And Moses said unto the Lord, See, thou sayest unto me, Bring up this people: and thou hast not let me know whom thou wilt send with me. Yet thou hast said, I know thee by name, and thou hast also found grace in my sight.

Now therefore, I pray thee, if I have found grace in thy sight, shew me now thy way, that I may know thee, that I may find grace in thy sight: and consider that this nation is thy people.

And he said, My presence shall go with thee, and I will give thee rest.

And he said unto him, If thy presence go not with me, carry us not up hence.

For wherein shall it be known here that I and thy people have found grace in thy sight? is it not in that thou goest with us?

so shall we be separated, I and thy people, from all the people that are upon the face of the earth.

And the Lord said unto Moses, I will do this thing also that thou hast spoken: for thou hast found grace in my sight, and I know thee by name.

And he said, I beseech thee, shew me thy glory.

ii. Prayer of Abraham, a man who negotiated with God

Genesis 18:17–22

And the LORD said, Shall I hide from Abraham that thing which I do;

Seeing that Abraham shall surely become a great and mighty nation, and all the nations of the earth shall be blessed in him?

For I know him, that he will command his children and his household after him, and they shall keep the way of the Lord, to do justice and judgment; that the Lord may bring upon Abraham that which he hath spoken of him.

And the Lord said, Because the cry of Sodom and Gomorrah is great, and because their sin is very grievous;

I will go down now, and see whether they have done altogether according to the cry of it, which is come unto me; and if not, I will know.

And the men turned their faces from thence, and went toward Sodom: but Abraham stood yet before the Lord.

EFFECTIVE PRAYERS ARE:

- **Fervent**

    Fervent (fire, zealous, keen) prayers are passionate and earnest pleadings with God.

HEBREWS 5:7

Who in the days of his flesh, when he had offered up prayers and supplications with strong crying and tears unto him that was able to save him from death, and was heard in that he feared.

JAMES 5:16

The effectual fervent prayer of a righteous man availeth much.

Prayers must be red-hot. Coldness of the spirit hinders praying.

- **Righteous**

PSALM 66:18

If I regard iniquity in my heart, the Lord will not hear me.

ISAIAH 59:1–2

Behold, the Lord's hand is not shortened, that it cannot save; neither his ear heavy, that it cannot hear:

But your iniquities have separated between you and your God, and your sins have hid his face from you, that he will not hear.

- **Persistent**

LUKE 18:1

And he spake a parable unto them to this end, that men ought always to pray, and not to faint.

You must not give up in prayer or quit because of a delay in receiving answers. Persistent and earnest prayer will eventually deliver the result expected. Don't allow the obstacles in the path of the answer intimidate you to surrender in defeat. Keep on asking, push on seeking, and knock harder; the answer is coming!

☑ When your heart is burdened and heavy...pray

PHILIPPIANS 4:6–7

Be careful for nothing; but in every thing by prayer and supplication with thanksgiving let your requests be made known unto God.
And the peace of God, which passeth all understanding, shall keep your hearts and minds through Christ Jesus.

☑ When you are gripped with fear of the foe...pray

ISAIAH 37:14–15

And Hezekiah received the letter from the hand of the messengers, and read it: and Hezekiah went up unto the house of the LORD, and spread it before the LORD.
And Hezekiah prayed unto the LORD.

☑ When you are at a junction of confusion and you don't know what to do...pray.

☑ When you are distressed and pressured by weight of a need... pray.

1 SAMUEL 1:9–10, 15

So Hannah rose up after they had eaten in Shiloh, and after they had drunk. Now Eli the priest sat upon a seat by a post of the temple of the LORD.

And she was in bitterness of soul, and prayed unto the LORD, and wept sore.
And Hannah answered and said, No, my lord, I am a woman of a sorrowful spirit: I have drunk neither wine nor strong drink, but have poured out my soul before the LORD.

God is a mere breath away. Prayer transports us into His presence immediately. Prayer is your answer to unfruitfulness, the answer to your weakness, and it is the key to a winning life. One thing to do when you don't know what else to do is pray.

The reason for such a lack of prayer today is because we don't believe it works.

In *Connecting with God*, Herb Miller tells the story of a nightclub opening on Main Street in a small town. Upon hearing the news, the only church in that town organized an all-night prayer meeting. The members asked God to burn down the club. Within a few minutes, lightning struck the club, and it burned to the ground. The club owner sued the church, which denied responsibility for the destruction of the club.

After hearing both sides, the judge said, "It seems that wherever the guilt may lie, the nightclub owner believes in prayer, while the church doesn't."

We are too busy, engrossed in our daily activities, and we misplace our priorities.

THE SECRETS OF PRAYER THAT MOVE GOD'S HAND
JOSHUA 10:12–14

Then spake Joshua to the LORD in the day when the LORD delivered up the Amorites before the children of Israel, and he said in the sight of Israel, Sun, stand thou still upon Gibeon; and thou, Moon, in the valley of Ajalon.
And the sun stood still, and the moon stayed, until the people had avenged themselves upon their enemies. Is not this written in the book of Jasher? So the sun stood still in the midst of heaven, and hasted not to go down about a whole day.

And there was no day like that before it or after it, that the LORD hearkened unto the voice of a man: for the LORD fought for Israel.

1. Pray persistently with unwavering faith.

Pray with confidence and conviction that answers to your prayers are coming.

LUKE 11:5–9

And he said unto them, Which of you shall have a friend, and shall go unto him at midnight, and say unto him, Friend, lend me three loaves;

For a friend of mine in his journey is come to me, and I have nothing to set before him?

And he from within shall answer and say, Trouble me not: the door is now shut, and my children are with me in bed; I cannot rise and give thee.

I say unto you, Though he will not rise and give him, because he is his friend, yet because of his importunity he will rise and give him as many as he needeth.

And I say unto you, Ask, and it shall be given you; seek, and ye shall find; knock, and it shall be opened unto you.

1 KINGS 18:41–45

And Elijah said unto Ahab, Get thee up, eat and drink; for there is a sound of abundance of rain.

So Ahab went up to eat and to drink. And Elijah went up to the top of Carmel; and he cast himself down upon the earth, and put his face between his knees,

And said to his servant, Go up now, look toward the sea. And he went up, and looked, and said, There is nothing. And he said, Go again seven times.

And it came to pass at the seventh time, that he said, Behold, there ariseth a little cloud out of the sea, like a man's hand. And he said, Go up, say unto Ahab, Prepare thy chariot, and get thee down, that the rain stop thee not.

And it came to pass in the mean while, that the heaven was black with clouds and wind, and there was a great rain. And Ahab rode, and went to Jezreel.

2. Pray in the Spirit.

ROMANS 8:26–27

Likewise the Spirit also helpeth our infirmities: for we know not what we should pray for as we ought: but the Spirit itself maketh intercession for us with groanings which cannot be uttered. And he that searcheth the hearts knoweth what is the mind of the Spirit, because he maketh intercession for the saints according to the will of God,

JUDE 1:21

Keep yourselves in the love of God, looking for the mercy of our Lord Jesus Christ unto eternal life.

When we pray in tongues; we make a direct contact with God without any hindrance; that is, our spirit links with the Holy Spirit. You speak mysteries to God that neither man nor Satan understands (1 Corinthians 14:2). You edify or build up yourself spiritually, and you bring distraction to the barest level in prayer.

3. Pray with a vow.

PSALM 50:14–15

Offer unto God thanksgiving; and pay thy vows unto the most High: And call upon me in the day of trouble: I will deliver thee, and thou shalt glorify me.

GENESIS 28:20–22

And Jacob vowed a vow,(in Bethel) saying, If God will be with me, and will keep me in this way that I go, and will give me bread to eat, and raiment to put on, So that I come again to my father's house in peace; then shall the LORD be my God: And this stone, which I have set for a pillar, shall be God's house: and of all that thou shalt give me I will surely give the tenth unto thee.

A vow can strengthen our hands in prayer. It can become an anchor to hang our petitions on in a difficult and overwhelming situation. Holy men and women in the Bible used vows to secure answers to their prayers, as we see in Jacob when he was running away from Esau, Hannah when she was desperate for a child, and Jonah when he was in the belly of the fish.

You can include a vow in your prayer when you are in a desperate moment of life. However, be aware that vows should not be entered into when the subject of your prayer is contrary to the will of God. A vow is not a bribe. It is like a catalyst to stimulate your faith and your prayer.

4. Pray with fasting.

The impeding danger Esther and the Jews faced in days of Mordecai made them declare three days of fasting and prayer (Esther 4:3). When Jehoshaphat faced a large host of army, he also called for a fast.

2 CHRONICLES 20:3

And Jehoshaphat feared, and set himself to seek the LORD, and proclaimed a fast throughout all Judah.

When you are faced with demonic opposition, it is time to fast.

MATTHEW 17:21

Howbeit this kind goeth not out but by prayer and fasting.

5. Pray prayers that are focused and premised on the Word.

Learn to connect your petitions and requests with God's written Word. The Word of God is the mind of God; you cannot go wrong in prayer when you pray His mind. God and His Word cannot be separated, and He always honors His Word and promises when we meet the conditions attached to them.

PRAYER AND WARFARE: WRESTLING WITH DARK ANGELS

We very often face stiff resistance and opposition to our prayer. Such opposition is engineered in the spiritual realm by wicked forces with a mission to delay or hinder the answer to our petitions. Daniel faced a problem like this in Daniel 12. A demonic principality referred to as the "Prince of Persia" stood against the answer.

Life is fragile—handle with prayer.

REVELATION 12:7–8

And there was war in heaven: Michael and his angels fought against the dragon; and the dragon fought and his angels,
And prevailed not; neither was their place found any more in heaven.

MARK 3:27

No man can enter into a strong man's house, and spoil his goods, except he will first bind the strong man; and then he will spoil his house.

Remember some doors are closed and kept by "strong men." It will take powerful, prevailing prayers to displace them.

Prayer is measured by its depth, not its length.

Keep a secret and it is yours; tell it to God and it's prayer; tell it to people and it's gossip.

The tragedy of our day is not unanswered prayer but unoffered prayer.

Satan: Blessed is he who has no time to pray, for he will become an easy prey. –Encyclopedia of 15,000 Illustrations

BLIND BARTIMAEUS

THIS IS IT OR NEVER!

"And when he heard that it was Jesus of Nazareth, he began to cry out, and say, Jesus, thou Son of David, have mercy on me" (Mark 10:47).

BARTIMAEUS: A MAN WITH 20/20 VISION

Blind Bartimaeus gives us a good example of how to get help from God. When he cried out to Christ for help, Christ heard his cry and healed Bartimaeus of his blindness. Not everyone who cries to God gets this sort of response. The reason is that they do not cry aright. We note four things about the cry of Bartimaeus that made it an effective cry. They are the listening before the cry, the loudness of the cry, the lauding in the cry, and the lowliness in the cry.

20/20 SPIRITUAL SIGHT:

Bartimaeus saw a possibility in a hopeless situation…the possibility of faith. He saw his healing first before he received it. He saw opportunity and recognized the right moment. Jesus might never pass that way again, so he seized the moment. Many people saw the crowd, heard the noise, and enjoyed the excitement. But you only see what you are looking for. Bartimaeus saw an opportunity of a lifetime.

In adversity and our challenges, do we see any opportunity? Your problem can also be the solution. The rod was a burden for Moses; it was also the instrument for the miraculous. Our pain and trials also work for us only if we can see beyond them.

Bartimaeus saw that his time had come; his moment of deliverance was now. That was why he was persistent. He saw it in his spirit, and no one was going to distract him or shout him down. What you see becomes the basis of your conviction. Some see opportunity in the adversity while others only see adversity in their opportunity.

A salesman was once sent by his company to a foreign nation to market shoes. He wired his manufacturer, "I want to come home. Nobody wears shoes in this part of Africa." So they brought him home and sent another salesman who shipped back order after order. He wrote the home office, "Everybody here needs shoes!"

In the prayer of Bartimaeus, we first observe *the listening before the cry*: "When he heard that it was Jesus of Nazareth." The attentive listening by Bartimaeus is a good example of using our opportunities. He could not look because he was blind, but he could listen. He used what he had. Be a good steward of what you have, and you will get more. God does not give more to those who do not use what they already have.

Many of us don't listen before we fire on in prayer...then we misfire. For your prayer to be effective, you need to practice the art of listening to the Spirit of God within you. Don't just open your mouth and say something; let the Holy Spirit give you the prayer points. After you are done praying, it is also a good practice to wait a moment before you rush out of His presence. Perhaps He has something to tell you about what you just asked Him. Often we miss out on this important part of prayer because we are in such a hurry to pass our burden across to God and we fail to realize He also wants to talk to us. Prayer is meant to be a conversation between two parties, not "one-way traffic."

ECCLESIASTES 5:1
Keep thy foot when thou goest to the house of God, and be more ready to hear, than to give the sacrifice of fools: for they consider not that they do evil.

JAMES 1:19
Wherefore, my beloved brethren, let every man be swift to hear, slow to speak, slow to wrath.

Second, in his prayer, we notice *the loudness of the cry*: "He began to cry out." The word translated "cry out" can be translated "scream," for it is that strong of a word. The loudness of the cry demonstrates the earnestness of the appeal. With a great crowd around Christ, it was necessary to appeal loudly to be heard. If you are not earnest in crying to God for help, do not expect God to be earnest in giving you help.

God not only respond to our prayers, but He is also interested in the passion we engage in prayer...the earnestness we put into it that makes us engage in fasts, waking up in the wee hours of the night, and so on.

JAMES 5:16

Confess your faults one to another, and pray one for another,
that ye may be healed. The effectual fervent ("earnest, heartfelt"
[AMP]) prayer of a righteous man availeth much.

This does not mean God will not hear whispers of prayer. There are moments when we are not in a place where we can shout or cry out loud. God's ears are not "heavy" to hear our moaning, our sighing, or even the prayer we mutter under our breath (Isaiah 59:1). The emphasis is not on how loud but how passionate we are in prayer. When we are desperate like Bartimaeus, we don't care who is around us or listening to our prayer.

Then we notice *the lauding in the cry*: "Jesus, thou Son of David." This cry honored Christ because it called Him "Son of David." This term said Christ was the promised Messiah; He was the King of Israel. If you want help from God, you need to honor God. If your prayers are not doing much good, maybe the reason is that you are not giving much honor to God in your prayers.

Bartimaeus demonstrated knowledge in his cry. He identified Jesus correctly while many who have their 20/20 physical vision failed and refused to acknowledge the title and person of Christ. Correct knowledge always empowers prayer. It is always an advantage in prayer to arm yourself with God's promises and knowledge of God's will as revealed in His Word before you embark on your prayer journey. Prayer is more potent when it is premised on God's truth.

Finally, we see *the Lowliness in the cry*: "Have mercy on me." Bartimaeus took the proper position before Christ. He did not plead merit, but he pleaded mercy. If we come on the basis of merit, we will not get much, for in God's sight and evaluation, we have no merit of note. You will get more from God pleading mercy than merit. It may be humbling to come to God pleading mercy. But it is the only way to appeal to Him successfully.

Our access to God's throne is made possible by His mercy through Christ our Lord; so is our stand before Him. The place we meet God is called the "seat of mercy" as He gave it to Moses.

EXODUS 25:22

And there I will meet with thee, and I will commune with thee from above the mercy seat, from between the two cherubims which are upon the ark of the testimony, of all things which I will give thee in commandment unto the children of Israel.

Whatever situation in our lives, when wrapped around with pleadings of mercy, will always get God's attention.

HEBREWS 4:16

Let us therefore come boldly unto the throne of grace, that we may obtain mercy, and find grace to help in time of need.

When we obtain mercy first, we will find grace to help us accomplish whatever we present before His throne.

THE IMPORTUNITY OF BARTIMAEUS
MARK 10:46–48

And they came to Jericho: and as he went out of Jericho with his disciples and a great number of people, blind Bartimaeus, the son of Timaeus, sat by the highway side begging. And when he heard that it was Jesus of Nazareth, he began to cry out, and say, Jesus, thou Son of David, have mercy on me. And many charged him that he should hold his peace: but he cried the more a great deal, Thou Son of David, have mercy on me.

His deliverance was more important than his dignity; getting his sight was better than looking good. Unusual acts on our part capture God's attention. Your persistence in crying and calling will get God on your side if you don't give up.

THE POWER OF PERSISTENT PRAYER

Perseverance in the place of prayer is a vital key to a winning life.

LUKE 18:1

And he spake a parable unto them to this end, that men ought always to pray, and not to faint.

The word *faint* means "to give up, lose heart, surrender to defeat." The dictionary meaning of *perseverance* includes "persistence, pertinacity, tenaciousness, and determination."

> *A man is not finished when he is defeated. He is finished when he quits.*

No matter how bad your situation might seem, no matter how hopeless the circumstances or how helpless you might feel, don't lose heart. It may seem like God is far away and has abandoned you, but that is never the case. Instead, God wants you to learn how to persevere in your faith.

Perseverance wins all the time. No matter how long and how tough the battle is, give it perseverance and you will win. The main secret of winning life's battles lies in persistence, the ability to stand when others fall under pressure. When the road becomes rough and the future seems cloudy, one thing to do is to move on.

You may fall seven times, but if you persevere, you will rise again. One of the best ways to give your best a chance is to rise up when you are knocked down. A man is not finished when he is defeated. He is finished when he quits.

RECOGNIZING YOUR OPPORTUNITY

Faith is full of inventions; faith does not look at circumstances. It sees a way in the midst of obstacles; it sees what others cannot. The tragedy of our days is that people have eyes but they cannot see. Bartimaeus recognized his season and the timing of his miracle. Some of the people in the crowd that day saw Jesus as the new prophet visiting town, but Bartimaeus saw Jesus as his "meal ticket" out of the misery of begging, and so he held fast to his cry.

This is the story of many people who lack vision. The Word says, "Where there is no vision, the people perish"; they waste away unfulfilled. A person without vision or purpose is walking through life like a blind man.

How far you can see with your eyes of faith is how far you can reach in life. What we see in faith is what we get, and what we eventually become. Ten out of the twelve spies Moses sent to search the land of Canaan could only see giants, defeat, and death. But Caleb and Joshua saw differently. They saw God and victory, they saw opportunity in adversity, and they were the only adult survivors to enter the Promised Land.

Every day God opens some new opportunities for many of us for something great. But some doors are being opened while others are closed. Unfortunately many of us travel through life with closed eyes and ears; we are not aware of what God is doing around us.

The hardest part of using opportunity in life is recognizing it. Often we realize great opportunities too late, when the door is closed on them. The citizens of Jesus' hometown had the first shot at His miracles, but they did not recognize Him as their Messiah, and they lost the opportunity to be healed and blessed.

MARK 6:5

And he could there do no mighty work, save that he laid his hands upon a few sick folk, and healed them.

Because we take things for granted, many of us miss great opportunities in life. Familiarity breeds contempt. What you fail to honor cannot bless you. Many people are blind to see the opportunities that God often sends their way. Some opportunities are wrapped in ugly, unattractive coverings. Many of the world's greatest men are people who cashed in on opportunities: Bill Gates, Donald Trump, etc. May God open your eyes, too.

Opportunities are often found in insignificant things, people, and places. Bethlehem was an insignificant place in Israel, yet it became Christ's birthplace. Nathaniel could not see any great thing coming out of there, and he almost missed the Savior (John 1:46).

The miracle of Naaman was locked up in a testimony of a little maid raided from Israel by Syrians. Her voice could have been despised as that of a slave girl and Naaman would have died a leper (2 Kings 5).

Everyone God places around our lives have their purpose. Some opportunities are locked inside a problem. God's open doors are often disguised as problems. There are opportunities in adversities: Your troubles can be your opportunities.

ROMANS 8:28

And we know that all things work together for good to them that love God, to them who are the called according to his purpose.

Without a Goliath, which showed up as a problem, David would have been an undiscovered talent and might never have fulfilled his destiny. Instead of whining and blaming, seek out a hidden message in what comes your way; your disappointment can eventually be a divine appointment.

The other day I ran across the story of a man who had a great opportunity that he missed. His friend took him for a ride one day way out in the country. They drove off the main road and into groves of trees to a large, uninhabited expanse of land. A few horses were grazing, and a couple of old shacks remained. The friend, Walter, stopped the car, got out, and started to describe with great vividness the wonderful things he was going to build. He wanted his friend Arthur to buy some of the land surrounding his project to get in on the ground floor.

But Arthur thought to himself, *Who in the world is going to drive twenty-five miles for this crazy project? The logistics of the venture are staggering.*

And so Walter explained to his friend Arthur, "I can handle the main project myself. But it will take all my money. But the land bordering it, where we're standing now, will in just a couple of years be jammed with hotels and restaurants and convention halls to accommodate the people who will come to spend their entire vacation here at my park." He continued, "I want you to have the first chance at this surrounding acreage, because in the next five years it will increase in value several hundred times."

And so Art Linkletter turned down the opportunity to buy up all the land that surrounded what was to become Disneyland. His friend, Walt Disney, had tried to talk him into it. But Art thought he was crazy.

CRY FOR MERCY

The cry for mercy always touches God's heart in a special way, regardless of who is making the cry. God's riches and blessings are made available to all on the platform of His grace and mercy. When sinners call for Him, He responds graciously, as seen in the parable Jesus gave of the publican who went to the temple to pray. He did not plead on his merit or achievement as the Pharisee did; he simply begged God for mercy. He went home justified (Luke 18:10–14).

The word *mercy* is from the Hebrew word *hesed*, which means "mercy, love, loving kindness." Mercy is compassion in action. Mercy and grace should not be confused; they are close but not the same in meaning. Mercy brings relief from punishment. Grace offers pardon from the crime. In a medical sense, mercy eliminates the pain while grace cures the disease.

When you feel overwhelmed, cry out for the mercy of God. In your desperate moment, wrap your prayers with His mercy. When the enemy points his accusing finger to lay claim on a loved one, the one thing to do is to stake it out on the platform of the mercy of God. The cry for mercy will not be denied.

God's mercy is shown to us in many ways:

- ☑ His mercy brings pardon from our sins.
- ☑ By His mercy, He answers our prayers, not on our merit.
- ☑ In mercy He corrects us when we are wrong. His mercy compels Him to chastise us when we miss the mark so that we might not miss heaven.
- ☑ His favor and tender love are released to us through the medium of His mercy.

David understood the power of God's mercy. In 2 Samuel 24:11–14, after he sinned, God gave him three options of punishment. He wisely threw himself onto the mercy hands of God, and God showed him mercy.

2 SAMUEL 24:10–14

And David's heart smote him after that he had numbered the people. And David said unto the LORD, I have sinned greatly in that I have done: and now, I beseech thee, O LORD, take away the iniquity of thy servant; for I have done very foolishly.
For when David was up in the morning, the word of the LORD came unto the prophet Gad, David's seer, saying,
Go and say unto David, Thus saith the LORD, I offer thee three things; choose thee one of them, that I may do it unto thee.
So Gad came to David, and told him, and said unto him, Shall seven years of famine come unto thee in thy land? or wilt thou flee three months before thine enemies, while they pursue thee? or that there be three days' pestilence in thy land? now advise, and see what answer I shall return to him that sent me.
And David said unto Gad, I am in a great strait: let us fall now into the hand of the LORD; for his mercies are great: and let me not fall into the hand of man.

HOW TO RECEIVE GOD'S MERCY IN LIFE

1. By humility. A proud heart cannot receive mercy. God resists the proud and gives grace to the humble, (See 1 Peter 5:5.)
2. Cut yourself off from the things you depend on in life. Mercy is released at our desperate moment, when we have renounced confidence in the arm of flesh and fully put our trust in Him.
3. By pleadings in prayer and the intercessions of others for us. The psalmist cried for it in Psalm 86:3.
4. By showing mercy to others. "Blessed are the merciful for they shall obtain mercy" (Matthew 5:7).

Dispense mercy generously to other people who desire your mercy. Sow the seed of mercy and you will reap it everywhere you go.

CARING FOR FAMILY'S KILLER

In 1946, Czeslaw Godlewski was a member of a young gang that roamed and sacked the German countryside. On an isolated farm they gunned down ten members of the Wilhelm Hamelmann family. Nine of the victims died, but Hamelmann himself survived his four bullet wounds. Godlewski recently completed a twenty-year prison term for his crimes, but the state would not release him because he had nowhere to go. When Hamelmann learned of the situation, he asked the authorities to release Godlewski into his custody. He wrote in his request, "Christ died for my sins and forgave me. Should I not then forgive this man?"
—Gospel Herald

That is true mercy on display.

Chapter 3

THE PLEADINGS OF HANNAH

PUSHING THROUGH THE BARRIERS
(1 SAMUEL 1:1-20; 2:1-10)

HANG ON, THE ANSWER IS COMING!

Hannah means favored, gracious. Yet her name did not directly translate into a miracle. God was making her wait. God's plan for her was great, but God was not in a hurry to release it. Sometimes we see people who are not living right are getting all the blessings and those who are dedicated to God seemingly forgotten. Penninah got all the blessings for a time.

1 SAMUEL 1:5
But unto Hannah he gave a worthy portion; for he loved Hannah: but the LORD had shut up her womb.

The Lord knew about her challenges. He sometimes allows circumstances like this to try our faith, establish His glory, and bless His people.

Why does a good God allow bad things (difficulties) to happen to good people? Because God has an eternal focus in mind, not temporal blessings, which are often our focus. He sometimes needs to prepare us for such a time so that we can handle the blessings.

WHAT ON EARTH IS THE PURPOSE OF TRIALS?
DEUTERONOMY 8:2
And thou shalt remember all the way which the LORD thy God led thee these forty years in the wilderness, to humble thee, and to prove thee, to know what was in thine heart, whether thou wouldest keep his commandments, or no.

The problems you face will either defeat you or develop you, depending on how you respond to them. Unfortunately, most people fail to see how God wants to use problems for good in their lives. They react foolishly and resent their problems rather than pausing to consider what benefit they might bring.

Every cross God allows us to carry in life has some temporal or eternal purpose, either for our own good or for the good of others. Here is a lesson for all mankind! A man's burden can become a bridge for his progress.

The popular author Tommy Higle has identified four ways God can use problems in the life of a believer:

TO DIRECT US

God can use problems to direct us away from sin, temptations, and bad decisions we are about to make. Sometimes God must light a fire under you to get you moving. Problems often point us in a new direction and motivate us to change. Is God trying to get your attention? *"Sometimes it takes a painful situation to make us change our ways" (Proverbs 20:30 GNT).*

I love the illustration I once read about Wallace Johnson, builder of numerous Holiday Inn motels and convalescent hospitals. Here in his own words:

> "When I was forty years old. I worked in a sawmill. One morning the boss told me. 'You're fired!' Depressed and discouraged, I felt like the world had caved in on me. It was during the Depression, and my wife and I greatly needed the small wages I had been earning.
>
> When I went home, I told my wife what had happened. She asked, 'What are you going to do now?' I replied, 'I'm going to mortgage our little home, and go into the building business.'
>
> My first venture was the construction of two small buildings. Within five years, I was a multimillionaire! Today, if I could locate the man who fired me, I would sincerely thank him for what he did. At the time it happened, I didn't understand why I was fired. Later, I saw that it was God's unerring and wondrous plan to get me into the way of His choosing!"

TO INSPECT US

It has been said that people are like teabags: If you want to know what's inside of them, just drop them into hot water. Has God ever tested your faith with a problem? What do problems reveal about you? Can we trust Him in pains and disappointments?

You may have thought you were strong until God brought a situation that made you panic. Every bridge designed to bear a heavy burden must first be tested before it opens for traffic.

Before God allows millions to pass into your hands, He first tests your attitude to the few dollars you hoard in your pocket. Your struggles and trials of now are God's "time paper" to determine your placement tomorrow. If you fail, you repeat the class. Make up your mind to pass no matter what.

TO CORRECT US

PSALM 23:4

Yea, though I walk through the valley of the shadow of death, I will fear no evil: for thou art with me; thy rod and thy staff they comfort me.

The shepherd's rod and staff are sources of **comfort, protection, and guidance**. Whenever necessary He may use the rod for **correction** also.

Some lessons we learn only through pain and failure. It is likely that as a child, your parents told you not to touch a hot stove. But you probably learned by being burned. Sometimes we only learn the value of something—health, money, or a relationship—by losing it.

PSALM 119:71–72 (TLB)

The punishment you gave me was the best thing that could have happened to me, for it taught me to pay attention to your laws. They are more valuable to me than millions in silver and gold!

The storm that Jonah faced took out the stubbornness in him. Many are opposed to correction. They get annoyed when their errors are pointed out. Sermons preached by their pastors offend them. The quickest way to destruction is to think one knows all.

David's sin of adultery was rewarded with STDs (sexually transmitted diseases).

PSALM 38:5, 7

My wounds stink and are corrupt because of my foolishness. For my loins are filled with a loathsome disease: and there is no soundness in my flesh.

Some who will not listen by any other means to correction need the spanking of God. Must God spank you before you change? If God must use difficulty to save us from ourselves, He will not hesitate.

TO PERFECT US

When responded to correctly, problems are character-builders. God is far more interested in our character than our comfort. Your relationship to God and your character are the only two things you are going to take with you into eternity.

ROMANS 5:3–4
And not only so, but we glory in tribulations also: knowing that tribulation worketh patience; and patience, experience; and experience, hope.

If you have problem with patience, God may place someone around you who provokes and aggravates you until you learn long-suffering. If yours is a lack of love, He throws someone your way who is difficult to love.

Without character, your Christianity is meaningless. God often uses tough situations to bring out the gems in us.

EAGLE TEACHES EAGLETS TO FLY

When an eagle wants to teach its little ones to fly from the nest high upon a cliff, hundreds of feet up in the air, it prods one of the little eaglets, and with its beak, noses it out of the nest. The eaglet starts to fall, and the great eagle flies underneath, puts its wing out, catches the little one on its back, and flies a mile into the air.

When you can hardly see the eagle as a point in the sky, it turns sideways, and down falls the little eaglet, which goes fluttering maybe a thousand feet.

Meanwhile, the eagle circles around the eaglet and underneath it, the eagle catches the eaglet on its wings and carries the eaglet up in the air again. After dishing the eaglet out again and letting it go, the eaglet comes down farther and farther—sometimes within a hundred feet of the ground.

Again the great eagle catches the little one on its back and up they go another mile. Little by little the eaglet will learn how to fly. The eagle knows when the eaglet is tired; it spoons the eaglet into the nest, noses out the next one and starts off again. —Donald Grey Barnhouse (Encyclopedia of 15,000 Illustrations)

1 SAMUEL 1:6–7
And her adversary also provoked her sore, for to make her fret, because the LORD had shut up her womb. And as he did so year by year, when she went up to the house of the LORD, so she provoked her; therefore she wept, and did not eat.

The devil takes special interest in provoking us into anxiety, impatience, and unnecessary self-pity. He becomes excited when we are depressed, down, and sad. We must understand his strategy and turn the tables against him.

1 SAMUEL 1:10–11
And she was in bitterness of soul, and prayed unto the LORD, and wept sore. And she vowed a vow, and said, O LORD of hosts, if thou wilt indeed look on the affliction of thine handmaid, and remember me, and not forget thine handmaid, but wilt give unto thine handmaid a man child, then I will give him unto the LORD all the days of his life, and there shall no razor come upon his head.

DELAYS IN PRAYER
Sometimes we face delays in getting answers to prayer. Hannah faced such a delay. Every year she cried unto God for her womb to open and have children, without getting the answer to her prayer. Delay is discouraging when answers to prayers are not forthcoming. We are tempted to quit praying on the subject and give up on our expectations. If we can just hold on in faith, the answer is coming.

Faith and patience are essential ingredients of prayer, especially when we feel the pressure of our challenges and we become desperate. God will work according to His own schedule; we cannot rush Him or force His hands. He is sovereign and His timing is always perfect. Delays can strengthen our faith and instill patience into our lives. Impatience can make us miss God and His plans for our lives.

> *Delay is NOT denial...*
> *Hang on—the answer is coming!*

PSALM 27:14
Wait on the LORD: be of good courage, and he shall strengthen thine heart: wait, I say, on the LORD.

KEYS TO HANNAH GETTING THE ANSWERS TO HER PRAYERS

First, she shifted from the selfish prayer of "Give me a child so I can show Penninah, or be like others" to "For Your glory and use, Lord."

Second, she used the power and efficacy of vows. It is not in every instance of prayer that we need to vow. Vows must not be seen as negotiation, tying God's hands, or replacing faith, fasting, and consistent prayer.

Third, she became more specific in her prayers. She wanted a male child, not just any child. She was persistent and did not quit as the years went by. She stopped keeping track of time. Stubborn situations like this demand stubborn and drastic treatment.

She prayed a heartfelt prayer. She communed with God in her spirit. It was not a routine and religious act, but it was real and from the heart.

1 SAMUEL 1:13–15
Now Hannah, she spake in her heart; only her lips moved, but her voice was not heard: therefore Eli thought she had been drunken. And Eli said unto her, How long wilt thou be

drunken? put away thy wine from thee. And Hannah answered and said, No, my lord, I am a woman of a sorrowful spirit: I have drunk neither wine nor strong drink, but have poured out my soul before the LORD.

Finally, she had strong, unwavering faith in God's servant and his word. When Eli made the pronouncement over her, she arose in faith and her sad countenance changed.

1 SAMUEL 1:17–18

Then Eli answered and said, Go in peace: and the God of Israel grant thee thy petition that thou hast asked of him. And she said, Let thine handmaid find grace in thy sight. So the woman went her way, and did eat, and her countenance was no more sad.

She took God at His word and placed her life in His hands, with absolute trust and confidence.

1 SAMUEL 1:19–20

And they rose up in the morning early, and worshipped before the LORD, and returned, and came to their house to Ramah: and Elkanah knew Hannah his wife; and the LORD remembered her. 20Wherefore it came to pass, when the time was come about after Hannah had conceived, that she bare a son, and called his name Samuel, saying, Because I have asked him of the LORD.

God never forgets His children who have been desperately crying unto Him. There is a fullness of time for every miracle. When your heart's desires meet the purpose of God's glory and intentions, He releases the blessings with ease.

Before the song of victory, there is usually a cry; before the glory comes, there is an unpleasant story. For everyone who will tarry in the place of prayer, a testimony is sure to come.

VOWS IN PRAYER

PSALM 76:11 (NKJV)
Make vows to the LORD your God, and pay them;
Let all who are around Him bring presents to Him who ought
to be feared.

PSALM 50:14–15
Offer unto God thanksgiving; and pay thy vows unto the most
High: And call upon me in the day of trouble: I will deliver
thee, and thou shalt glorify me.

A vow is a solemn promise that involves at least two parties; in
this case, the divine and the mortal man. It is binding on the person
who made it after his desire is fulfilled. It is greater than a promise
but less than a covenant. In prayer, it is not supposed to be a bribe or
a way of getting one's ambition contrary to God's will. A vow is of no
effect outside God's express will and counsel.

THE PLACE AND PURPOSE OF VOWS IN PRAYER
Although normal prayers of faith without vows get answered,
there are particular instances when a vow makes the difference in
prayer. One example is Hannah's case—she had been going to Shiloh
to offer prayers for a son for a long time, but her prayer was answered
in the year she added a vow in prayer. God recognized her vow and
performed a miracle in response. Oftentimes God gives a miraculous
answer to prayers that are connected with a vow.

What does a vow do?
- It acts like a catalyst to prayer.
- It often forms a basis of pleading one's case before God (Psalm 51:11–15).
- It stimulates and elevates faith in God.
- It is a way of giving thanks to God after the answer (Psalm 50:14–15).

> ## *Vows can be made to break a stubborn habit!*

LINCOLN'S PROMISE TO MOTHER

While a member of Congress, Abraham Lincoln was once criticized by a friend for his seeming rudeness in declining to test the rare wines provided by their host.

The friend said to him: "There is certainly no danger of a man of your years and habits becoming addicted to the use of wine."

"I mean no disrespect, John," answered Lincoln, "but I promised my precious mother only a few days before she died that I would never use anything intoxicating as a beverage, and I consider that promise as binding today as it was the day I gave it."

"But," the friend continued, "there is a great difference between a child surrounded by a rough class of drinkers and a man in a home of refinement."

"A promise is a promise forever," answered Lincoln, "and when made to a mother, it is doubly binding."

–*Encyclopedia of 15,000 Illustrations*

Very often vows become operational and applicable when:

1. We desire a special miracle from God.

HANNAH'S VOW:

1 SAMUEL 1:10–11

And she was in bitterness of soul, and prayed unto the LORD, and wept sore. And she vowed a vow, and said, O LORD of hosts, if thou wilt indeed look on the affliction of thine hand-maid, and remember me, and not forget thine handmaid, but wilt give unto thine handmaid a man child, then I will give him unto the LORD all the days of his life, and there shall no razor come upon his head.

It is good for parents to make vows to God on behalf of their children; it may not be binding on the child but the parents to keep.

PROVERBS 31:1–2
The words of king Lemuel, the prophecy that his mother taught him. What, my son? and what, the son of my womb? and what, the son of my vows?

JONAH 1:15–16
So they took up Jonah, and cast him forth into the sea: and the sea ceased from her raging. Then the men feared the LORD exceedingly, and offered a sacrifice unto the LORD, and made vows.

JONAH 2:9–10
But I will sacrifice unto thee with the voice of thanksgiving; I will pay that that I have vowed. Salvation is of the LORD. And the LORD spake unto the fish, and it vomited out Jonah upon the dry land.

2. We are facing the impossible.

JACOB'S VOW

GENESIS 28:20–22
And Jacob vowed a vow,(in Bethel) saying, If God will be with me, and will keep me in this way that I go, and will give me bread to eat, and raiment to put on, So that I come again to my father's house in peace; then shall the LORD be my God: And this stone, which I have set for a pillar, shall be God's house: and of all that thou shalt give me I will surely give the tenth unto thee.

GENESIS 31:13
I am the God of Bethel, where thou anointedst the pillar, and where thou vowedst a vow unto me: now arise, get thee out from this land, and return unto the land of thy kindred.

PSALM 66:13–14
I will go into thy house with burnt offerings: I will pay thee my vows, which my lips have uttered, and my mouth hath spoken, when I was in trouble.

3. We attempt solving a peculiar life's problem.
Example: Jonah in the belly of the fish

JONAH'S VOW

Jonah was in deep trouble. After the disobedient prophet turned his back on God and took off in the opposite direction, he found himself in the belly of a fish. Three days passed and Jonah became very desperate. He wanted to get out by all means, which led to his desperate cry and vow in Jonah 2:

JONAH 2:1–2
Then Jonah prayed unto the LORD his God out of the fish's belly, And said, I cried by reason of mine affliction unto the LORD, and he heard me; out of the belly of hell cried I, and thou heardest my voice.

He concluded his prayer with a vow:
JONAH 2:9
But I will sacrifice unto thee with the voice of thanksgiving; I will pay that that I have vowed. Salvation is of the LORD.

CONDITIONS FOR MAKING VOWS

1. The desire to make a vow must be based primarily on God's Word and will. God is not bound by what is outside His counsel and eternal purpose. No vow on earth can force God to contravene His justice, righteousness, and eternal laws or what would not glorify Him now or in eternity; therefore, it is useless to make vows for such.

2. The vow must be redeemable; that is, it must be within our human capacity to fulfill it. Wisdom is needed in making vows. Rash decisions and uncertain vows must be avoided.

ECCLESIASTES 5:4–6
When thou vowest a vow unto God, defer not to pay it; for he hath no pleasure in fools: pay that which thou hast vowed. Better is it that thou shouldest not vow, than that thou should-

est vow and not pay. Suffer not thy mouth to cause thy flesh to sin; neither say thou before the angel, that it was an error: wherefore should God be angry at thy voice, and destroy the work of thine hands?

Three examples of rash vows:
a. Jephthah's awful vow—Judges 11:29–40
b. The vow of Israel—Judges 21:1, 5–6
c. The vow to death of forty men—Acts 23:12–14

ELEMENTS IN VOWS [WHAT WE CAN VOW]

What vows entail may vary from real and tangible substance to intangibles. Below are some examples:

☑ Praise, thanksgiving—Psalm 51:14–15; Jonah 2:9

☑ Dedication of self, substance, or articles to God—Genesis 28:20–22

☑ Monetary substances

☑ Our life, time to the service of God—1 Samuel 1:10–11, 27–28; Numbers 6:2–8

IMPLICATIONS OF UNREDEEMED (UNFULFILLED) VOWS

A vow must be specific. To vow is voluntary, so no one should be compelled.

NUMBERS 30:2

If a man vow a vow unto the LORD, or swear an oath to bind his soul with a bond; he shall not break his word, he shall do according to all that proceedeth out of his mouth.

NUMBERS 30:2 (TLB)

That when anyone makes a promise to the Lord, either to do something or to quit doing something, that vow must not be broken: the person making the vow must do exactly as he has promised.

To not fulfill a vow is a sin.
DEUTERONOMY 23:21 (NKJV)
When you make a vow to the LORD your God, you shall not delay to pay it; for the LORD your God will surely require it of you, and it would be sin to you.

It is an insult to God.
LEVITICUS 22:23 (NKJV)
Either a bull or a lamb that has any limb too long or too short you may offer as a freewill offering, but for a vow it shall not be accepted.

It becomes a breach of agreement. We may lose the miracle.

EXAMPLES OF PEOPLE/GROUPS WHO VOWED IN THE SCRIPTURES:
- Jacob's vow: Genesis 28:20–22
- Hannah's vow: 1 Samuel 1:11, 27–28
- Job's vow with his eyes: Job 31:1
- David's vow: Psalm 132:2–5
- Jephthah's vow: Judges 11:29–40
- Jonah's vow: Jonah 2:9
- Paul's vow: Acts 18:18
- The vow to death of 40 men: Acts 23:12

FULLNESS OF TIME
In God's program for His people, there is what is called the "fullness of time." Sometimes God makes us wait to receive a miracle because the time for it is not ripe. Blessings released to us before God's appointed time may not bring us many benefits; in fact, they may even be harmful to our lives.

The story of Joseph in prison can help us to grasp this fact (see Genesis 40). Two men who worked for Pharaoh, the king of Egypt, offended their master and were put in the prison, where they met Joseph. Both of them had unique dreams that Joseph interpreted: one was killed (the baker), and the other was released (the butler). Joseph made the butler promise to mention him to the king so as to gain his release from prison; unfortunately the man forgot his promise for two years. Afterward the king had a dream no one could interpret, which prompted the memory of the butler to remember his promise to Joseph.

What if the butler had remembered Joseph two years earlier immediately after his release from prison? Joseph probably would have been set free to go back to his family in Canaan, and he would not have been there to interpret for the king. The forgetfulness of the butler had a divine purpose; Pharaoh would have a dream that no one could interpret and it would be two years after the release of the butler. So Joseph had to wait for the fullness of time.

Is God making you wait? The delay may be to serve a greater purpose than what you thought. In God's fullness of time, He will make all things beautiful for you.

God has a schedule and the perfect timing for all His programs on earth. His plans for your life are on schedule. Don't panic. God's plan for your life will not fail. It may appear late on your own schedule, but not on His timetable! Nothing works until the appointed time He has chosen; all efforts prior to it will simply be frustrating.

GENESIS 18:14
Is anything too hard for the LORD? At the time appointed I will return unto thee, according to the time of life, and Sarah shall have a son.

GENESIS 21:2
For Sarah conceived, and bare Abraham a son in his old age, at the set time of which God had spoken to him.

There is an appointed time, also known as the "set time" for every divine intervention to manifest. Your Isaac ("laughter") will show up at the time appointed. It may look like He has forgotten you, but He did not. You will have the last laugh and the best laugh.

ISAIAH 49:14–16

But Zion said, The LORD hath forsaken me, and my Lord hath forgotten me. Can a woman forget her sucking child, that she should not have compassion on the son of her womb? yea, they may forget, yet will I not forget thee. Behold, I have graven thee upon the palms of my hands; thy walls are continually before me.

What are the dangers in jumping ahead of God?
1. We will miss God and His perfect purpose.
2. We will go in our own strength, without His support.
3. We may find ourselves in grave danger and can even get killed.

He will never be too early or too late for a rescue. God's delays always have a divine and hidden purpose. God is not slow; He only works by His timetable (see 2 Peter 3:8–9).

He is the Great Architect of the universe. He is orderly and organized. He never puts the cart before the horse. The divine time is always a perfect time, free of struggles and frustrations.

ECCLESIASTES 3:11

He hath made everything beautiful in his time: also he hath set the world in their heart, so that no man can find out the work that God maketh from the beginning to the end.

It will only be beautiful in the right time. Whatever is ugly now in your life indicates that the time of manifestation is not yet; at the fullness of time, it will turn to beauty.

Chapter 4

DESPERATE HEZEKIAH

THE PRAYER OF A DYING MAN: "LORD, I AM NOT READY!"

A STRUGGLE FOR SURVIVAL
2 KINGS 20:1–7

In those days was Hezekiah sick unto death. And the prophet Isaiah the son of Amoz came to him, and said unto him, Thus saith the LORD, Set thine house in order; for thou shalt die, and not live. Then he turned his face to the wall, and prayed unto the LORD, saying, I beseech thee, O LORD, remember now how I have walked before thee in truth and with a perfect heart, and have done that which is good in thy sight. And Hezekiah wept sore. And it came to pass, afore Isaiah was gone out into the middle court, that the word of the LORD came to him, saying, Turn again, and tell Hezekiah the captain of my people, Thus saith the LORD, the God of David thy father, I have heard thy prayer, I have seen thy tears: behold, I will heal thee: on the third day thou shalt go up unto the house of the LORD. And I will add unto thy days fifteen years; and I will deliver thee and this city out of the hand of the king of Assyria; and I will defend this city for mine own sake, and for my servant David's sake. And Isaiah said, Take a lump of figs. And they took and laid it on the boil, and he recovered.

Have you ever had a situation on your hands when you were confronted with a life-or-death matter, a close call, or a time when your options were limited? This is similar to what Hezekiah was facing—he was face-to-face with death. His dreams and plans were about to go unfulfilled.

In such situations, there are just two options: give up, surrender to fate, and patiently wait for death; or take up the challenge and fight.

Many times our lot in life and the outcomes of battles depend on us. It is our destiny; we have it in our hands: We can change things by the power of desperate and determined prayers.

Three things to do:

1. Learn to confront the fear.
2. Set aside the "whys and why not's".
3. Set your eyes on God, who can change the situation.

Prayer can change things, even death. What we lack in life can be as a result of insufficient prayer. When tough situations come against you, come against them with the weapon of prayer.

Then he turned his face to the wall, and prayed unto the Lord (2 *Kings 20:2*).

He cut himself off from the help and trust in man and relied solely on God through humility, submission, and yielding totally before God.

I beseech thee, O Lord, remember now how I have walked before thee in truth and with a perfect heart, and have done that which is good in thy sight. And Hezekiah wept sore (2 Kings 20:3).

He pleaded his case before God and reasoned with Him. "Remember now"—there must be some grounds or scriptural support to plead your case:

- His walk: godly walk and devotions to God
- His heart: perfect, faithful to God
- His deeds: a life of service, commitment, and consistency

Hezekiah spoke few words (just thirty) that lasted only a few minutes, but they yielded great results. Something about his life provoked God to action. Behind an effective prayer is the character and quality of life of the individual. Does your life command God's attention like the blood of Abel cried out to God?

He "wept sore." He poured his heart out to God. Those tears contained many unknown and unspoken requests that only God could understand.

And it came to pass, afore Isaiah was gone out into the middle court, that the word of the Lord came to him, saying. Turn again, and tell Hezekiah the captain of my people, Thus saith the Lord, the God of David thy father, I have heard thy prayer, I have seen thy tears: behold, I will heal thee: on the third day thou shalt go up unto the house of the Lord (2 *Kings 20:4–5*).

Answers can be quick or slow. God decides how, when, and in what means to answer us.

God heard his prayer, represented by his cry, and saw his tears, which were an expression of his pain.

What if he had not prayed?

First, he would have had no descendant or heir to carry on the name of David and the lineage of the Messiah.

MATTHEW 1:10

And Ezekias begat Manasses; and Manasses begat Amon; and Amon begat Josias.

The strength of our prayer lies in the covenant and promises of God. If you can locate His Word, it becomes the ground and basis to plead...and God is committed to His Word.

Second, he would have died prematurely. The devil wanted to shorten his life through the affliction of boils; therefore, he would have died not fulfilling his destiny.

Third, his nation would have been robbed of victory over Assyria. Certain things will not happen until we pray, even when that thing is the will of God for us.

The woman with issue of blood would have died in the pool of her own blood if she had not acted on her faith. But for the concern and desperate effort of some four friends during the ministry days of Jesus, one man would never have received his healing.

Prayer moves mountains. Our laziness in prayer can affect matters of life and death. If you think, *God will do whatever He wants to do in my life regardless if I pray or not*, you are wrong! Through our prayers, we can move God to change things in our lives.

TERMINAL CASES

Do you or a relative have a terminal disease? For some, it is cancer, HIV, heart diseases, or some serious disability. Your physician has written it up as impossible and has closed your file. Family and friends may have even given you up for death. Pastors and priests have fasted and prayed on the case, and the situation looks like that of Hezekiah.

Cheer up; there is one more appeal you can file. Bring the matter before heaven's courtroom and ask the Judge of the Universe to consider the case. Jesus, our Advocate, is ever willing to represent you before the Father. Hezekiah did exactly that: When all help failed, he took his case directly to the court of heaven and appealed the verdict. He turned his face from friends and foes; he turned to God alone.

ISAIAH 41:21
Produce your cause, saith the LORD; bring forth your strong reasons, saith the King of Jacob.

ISAIAH 43:26
Put me in remembrance: let us plead together: declare thou, that thou mayest be justified.

Friends, nothing is over until God says so. Appeal to the court of heaven, pour your heart to God, and give Him "strong reasons" to spare your life as Hezekiah did. God can turn the table around and give you an extension of life. It is not a big deal to the Almighty to prolong days and add years to our lives; He did it before. Plead your case as lawyers do in earthly courts pointing to this *precedence* in His Holy Word.

Nothing is terminal because men say so. Until God says so, fight on…desperately!

> *What we lack in life can be as a result of insufficient prayer. What you have not received may be what you have not asked.*

HOPE FOR THE HOPELESS
The way out of hopelessness is to turn your eyes to the Lord.

PSALM 34:5
They looked unto him, and were lightened: and their faces were not ashamed.

There is misery and hopelessness in our world. Every day count-less souls give up and commit suicide. They are sick and tired of their troubles and have lost hope completely. They did not know who else to turn to; they did not know the God to whom Hezekiah turned his face. The problem with modern believers is that we are looking—but not only unto Him. We look at other help and sources. Our look is divided between what we see and the promises of men and the Lord. If we are completely submersed in His light, darkness and shame cannot hide in our lives. Are your eyes on the hills or on the God of the hills? (See Psalm 121:1.)

Isaiah 45:22
Look unto me, and be ye saved, all the ends of the earth: for I am God, and there is none else.

FOUR WAYS YOU CAN LOOK
1. Look behind…see failure, disappointment, guilt, and con-demnation.
2. Look in front…see fear, worry, and hopelessness.
3. Look around…see discouragement, frustration, and helpless-ness.
4. Look upward, above…see Jesus, grace, and help.

The right place to look in our difficult and desperate situation is upward.

DON'T GIVE UP
Life is full of many discouraged people who thought they reached the end of their ropes. Their marriages failed, they went bankrupt in their businesses, they have been diagnosed with incurable diseases, their teenage kids ran away from home or are doing time in jail, and so on the list continues.

Here is a list of famous people who had bleak starts but went on to become successful because they refused to give up:

☑ Albert Einstein could not speak until he was four years old, and he did not read until he was seven.

- ☑ Beethoven's music teacher said about him: "As a composer he is hopeless."

- ☑ When Thomas Edison was a young boy, his teachers said he was so stupid he would never learn anything.

- ☑ Henry Ford forgot to put a reverse gear in his first car. He failed and went broke five times before he finally succeeded

- ☑ Walt Disney was fired by a newspaper editor for lack of ideas. Walt also went bankrupt several times before he built Disneyland.

- ☑ Abraham Lincoln failed several times and for many years his dreams did not materialize. He became one of the best presidents in America.

- ☑ Michael Jordan, perhaps the greatest basketball player of all time, did not make his high school basketball team his sophomore year.

- ☑ Winston Churchill failed the sixth grade. He did not become prime minister until he was sixty-two. His greatest contributions came when he was a "senior citizen."

Be encouraged. Hold on to hope. God can give you a break in your desperate situation. If it was not too late for God to give life to dry bones in the days of Ezekiel, your case is not hopeless (see Ezekiel 37).

A DEAD MAN CALLED LAZARUS

JOHN 11:1–3

Now a certain man was sick, named Lazarus, of Bethany, the town of Mary and her sister Martha. (It was that Mary which anointed the Lord with ointment, and wiped his feet with her hair, whose brother Lazarus was sick.) Therefore his sisters sent unto him, saying, Lord, behold, he whom thou lovest is sick.

Sickness is not limited to the physical bodies of men alone, but also to other areas of our lives. The world and the Church are full of sick people who need divine intervention to get them back on their feet. A man may be emotionally, financially, or spiritually sick. A job or home may be sick; in short, any area of your life where you are not functioning properly is sick. One's entire life may be sick. A man not born again is sick in his soul.

JOHN 11:38–41

Jesus therefore again groaning in himself cometh to the grave. It was a cave, and a stone lay upon it. Jesus said, Take ye away the stone. Martha, the sister of him that was dead, saith unto him, Lord, by this time he stinketh: for he hath been dead four days. Jesus saith unto her, Said I not unto thee, that, if thou wouldest believe, thou shouldest see the glory of God? Then they took away the stone from the place where the dead was laid. And Jesus lifted up his eyes, and said, Father, I thank thee that thou hast heard me.

Men had closed the life story of this man; family and friends had given up hope on him and they sealed his fate with a stone. Not only was Lazarus a dead problem, it had become a stinking problem. His case was hopeless; Jesus delayed His coming, He was late for Lazarus, and nothing could be done for him again, case closed!

But wait a minute. In the midst of wailing and weeping, the Master suddenly showed up. As far as heaven was concerned, Lazarus's file was not closed. Jesus stepped in; nothing is over until the God of the universe says so.

"Roll away the stone" was the Master's first action plan. For the touch of His miracles to reach you, certain stones must be removed:
- The stone of unbelief
- Self-pity and blaming others
- The hold of your past failure
- Unforgiveness and bitterness

All of these must be let go. Until you release them, heaven will not release your blessings.

JOHN 11:43–44

And when he thus had spoken, he cried with a loud voice, Lazarus, come forth. And he that was dead came forth, bound hand and foot with graveclothes: and his face was bound about with a napkin. Jesus saith unto them, Loose him, and let him go.

Jesus spoke to the dead as if it was living. He called Lazarus by his name, not as a corpse. Until you begin to call all the dead Lazaruses in your life by their proper names in faith, they will not be released from the dead. A Puritan writer said that if Jesus had not named Lazarus when He shouted, He would have emptied the whole cemetery!

Stop saying you are poor, miserable, and hopeless. Stand on His Word; keep His promises in your mouth. Decree and declare for your Lazarus to come forth. Your delay is not denial, but for God's glory to be revealed through you and in your desperate situation.

DON'T LOSE HOPE

Continue to hope for your miracle. There is power in hope. Hope sustains life; hopelessness is the shortcut to defeat.

Hope is a tonic that cheers the heart; when life is dark and difficult, we must not let go of the power of hope. Hope sustains life in its darkest hours and keeps us from sinking. When hope is gone, life is gone. Hang on to hope that all shall be well, that you will get married someday, that your health will get better, that your marriage will turn around.

Hope kept Abraham and Sarah sane in their delay (see Genesis 21:6–7). Hope kept Joseph's head above sorrow in jail. Job triumphed over calamities and trials by hope: "I know my redeemer liveth... though He slays me..."

We can hope in God's Word. We can hope in God's faithfulness.

PSALM 119:81

My soul fainteth for thy salvation: but I hope in thy word.

ELIJAH ON MOUNT CARMEL

RELEASING WHAT IS PROMISED

PROVOKE YOUR RAIN *through Effectual Fervent Prayer (James 5:16)*
1 KINGS 18:1
And it came to pass after many days, that the word of the LORD came to Elijah in the third year, saying, Go, shew thyself unto Ahab; and I will send rain upon the earth.

1 KINGS 18:41–46
And Elijah said unto Ahab, Get thee up, eat and drink; for there is a sound of abundance of rain. So Ahab went up to eat and to drink. And Elijah went up to the top of Carmel; and he cast himself down upon the earth, and put his face between his knees, And said to his servant, Go up now, look toward the sea. And he went up, and looked, and said, There is nothing. And he said, Go again seven times. And it came to pass at the seventh time, that he said, Behold, there ariseth a little cloud out of the sea, like a man's hand. And he said, Go up, say unto Ahab, Prepare thy chariot, and get thee down, that the rain stop thee not. And it came to pass in the mean while, that the heaven was black with clouds and wind, and there was a great rain. And Ahab rode, and went to Jezreel. And the hand of the LORD was on Elijah; and he girded up his loins, and ran before Ahab to the entrance of Jezreel.

It was a time of drought and dryness in the land for three and a half years. The heavens were locked; times were tough and lives were unbearable. The king of the land, Ahab, was desperate, and there was nothing he could do about it. A man called Elijah had locked the heavens and walked away with the keys, and it was going to require a fervent, diligent prayer to unlock them.

When your life, marriage, and business appear dry, it could mean a locked heaven. This necessitates a high gear of prayer to release refreshment. Lack of rain is an indication of a bigger problem: a shut-up heaven. Your cry today will be, "Open the floodgate of heaven; let it rain."

Though God has promised the rain, He still expects us to pray for it. Certain promises and prophetic utterances must be engaged through prayers and petitions for them to manifest. Elijah engaged the heavens for the land. It is not enough to receive a promise, fold our hands, and do nothing.

Rain represents:

- Blessings from God.
- Easement in time of dryness.
- Increase in the land.
- Outpouring of the power of the Spirit, which brings refreshment and comfort.

And Elijah said unto Ahab, Get thee up, eat and drink; for there is a sound of abundance of rain. So Ahab went up to eat and to drink. And Elijah went up to the top of Carmel; and he cast himself down upon the earth, and put his face between his knees (1 Kings 18:41–42).

Desperate moments of life when you need to provoke rainfall:

1. When victory eludes you and defeat seems imminent
2. When those who are to mock you have gathered as in the days of Elijah
3. When unbelievers are making fun of your faith, asking you where your God is
4. When evil powers are challenging God in your life
5. When you are beaten and battered in battle; when your nose is bleeding and your eyes are black in the boxing ring of life
6. When a satanic audience is waiting for your downfall
7. When you have looked at the whole of your family line and you don't want to follow its evil pattern
8. When you regularly shed tears of sorrow because of the desperate situation in which you constantly find yourself
9. When the road you are traveling is becoming rougher and rougher
10. When your life is a package of struggles and frustrations; when everything seems to be in disarray and nothing appears to be working

These are the kinds of troubles Elijah faced in his days. The nation had heard him made his boast of God; now they were waiting to see if God would reverse the dryness in the land. It was a desperate moment for him, and he engaged in desperate intercession.

HOW TO PROVOKE YOUR RAINFALL...

ASK FOR IT

ZECHARIAH 10:1
Ask ye of the LORD rain in the time of the latter rain; so the LORD shall make bright clouds, and give them showers of rain, to every one grass in the field.

TAKE OUT WORRY FROM YOUR LIFE

PHILIPPIANS 4:6 (NIV)
Do not be anxious about anything, but in everything, by prayer and petition, with thanksgiving, present your requests to God.

Worry introduces unneeded stress into our lives. It is based on "what if?" What if I lose my job, the citizenship application is denied, there is no one for me to marry in the world? Worry will give you something to do, but it won't get you anywhere. It is not your friend at all; rather, it is your enemy. Worry and faith are incompatible. Immediately, when worry runs in, faith jumps out. In other words, the beginning of worry is the end of faith.

I read about a doctor who once injected water (a placebo) into a patient who was agitating and complaining of symptoms of his sickness: "Give me medicine or I will die." After the administration, the patient said he felt better. His problem was in his mind.

Elijah declared there was rain before he saw it. Do you believe for what you're asking for in prayer? The answer to prayer can come from a small start. When you see the small hope...don't turn from it. The prayer of faith is the antidote to worry. Why worry when you can pray?

SACRIFICE AND WILLINGNESS TO PAY THE PRICE

Ahab went to eat and drink; Elijah went up to fast and agonize in prayer.

There is a price to pay for the release of the supernatural power of God. It is not in meat and drink; it comes by sacrifice. Before we can enjoy an abundance of rain in our lands, families, and finances, we must climb a "Mount Carmel" to meet with God and plead for the release.

Every new year is not automatically going to release an abundance of rain; we must go behind the curtain and plead with God.

Note the posture of Elijah in prayer: indicating pain before gain. Birth pangs of pain precede the delivery of our bundle of joy. The pain of fasting and prayer comes before the manifestation of a glorious future.

A RIGHTEOUS MAN

JAMES 5:16
Confess your faults one to another, and pray one for another, that ye may be healed. The effectual fervent prayer of a righteous man availeth much.

A right standing before God with our hearts washed constantly by the blood makes our cry to God effective and powerful. The prayer of a righteous man is powerful. It will dispossess and displace sin in your life. You should deal with strife and grudges before you offer your supplications.

PROVERBS 20:3 (MSG)
It's a mark of good character to avert quarrels, but fools love to pick fights.

IMPORTUNITY IN PRAYER

And said to his servant, Go up now, look toward the sea. And he went up, and looked, and said, There is nothing. And he said, Go again seven times. And it came to pass at the seventh time, that he said, Behold, there ariseth a little cloud out of the sea, like a man's hand. And he said, Go up, say unto Ahab, Prepare thy chariot, and get thee down, that the rain stop thee not (1 Kings 18:43–44).

Importunity and persistence is often required in some prayer issues. If you give up too quickly, you may lose the miracle. Pray until something happens. Paul prayed three times over the thorn in his flesh. Jesus prayed three times repeating same thing in the Garden before His death. Too many times we fail to get what God promised because we stop praying. Elijah held on to God's promise in prayer until the seventh time; he had a persistent, stubborn faith that would not accept defeat. Many people give up at the second or third effort.

FAITH IN THE PROMISES OF GOD
MARK 9:23

Jesus said unto him, If thou canst believe, all things are possible to him that believeth.

> *The shortest route to reach heaven is through prayer; the 'tallest' man on earth is the one on his knees.*

Elijah prayed in faith, for God told him He would send the rain (1 Kings 18:1). "Prayer," said Robert Law, "is not getting man's will done in heaven. It's getting God's will done on earth." You cannot separate the Word of God and prayer, for in His Word He gives us the promises that we claim when we pray. Never accept your present position as final. The reports from the bank or your physician are merely factual—the Word of God is truth.

Elijah was determined and concerned in his praying. "He prayed earnestly" (James 5:17, NIV). The Greek translation reads, "And he prayed in prayer." Many people do not pray in their prayers. They just lazily say religious words, and their hearts are not in their prayers.

ISAIAH 44:3
For I will pour water upon him that is thirsty, and floods upon the dry ground: I will pour my spirit upon thy seed, and my blessing upon thine offspring.

FIGHT IN PRAYER
1 TIMOTHY 1:18
This charge I commit unto thee, son Timothy, according to the prophecies which went before on thee, that thou by them mightest war a good warfare.

Why do we need to fight for what is already promised? After all, God has promised to send the rain (see 1 Kings 18:1), so, Elijah why are you struggling on the mountain?

First, the enemy will encroach on the blessing if we don't fight. For every new level God promised us, you can expect new devils to rise up with vehement anger. When God's Word is released into our lives as a prophecy or promise, it wakes up some demons who immediately begin to resist its fulfillment. That is why we must fight.

Many parents received great words over their children but never lived to see them fulfilled because they failed to watch over the word in prayer. If you receive a prophetic word into your life and fold your hands and become complacent about it, you may never see the fulfillment.

Second, the promise of God is as a good check; it is given by a God who cannot lie. But we have to take it to the bank to cash it. Prayer is "cashing" the checks of God's promises. Yes, you have the check in your possession, but what good does it do?

There was a story of an elderly woman who lived in Africa. Her son traveled to Britain to study and work. Over the years, the son sent her letters and money in pounds sterling. When the woman received them and looked at the currency notes, she saw the picture of the Queen of England on all of them. *My son is married to a beautiful white woman,* she thought and she filed the notes away in the cabinet. Years rolled by, and she continued to live in penury while receiving several hundreds of similar currency. *Why is my son sending me pictures of his wife again and again?* she thought. *He probably forgot he sent them already.* She filed them away. Finally her son returned one day and was shocked to see his mother living in poverty. The woman was angry that her son had neglected her and did not send her money—except for the "pictures of his wife," several thousands of pounds sterling neatly stored away in the cabinet while she suffered in penury. What ignorance!

We behave like this illiterate mother when we sit on great promises and don't fight for them. We must go to "Mount Carmel" and plead with God to release the rain that He promised.

Until you engage the enemy…

…your dreams will continue to slide.

…your rights will be denied.

…he will continue to steal from you.

ZECHARIAH 10:5

And they shall be as mighty men, which tread down their enemies in the mire of the streets in the battle: and they shall fight, because the LORD is with them, and the riders on horses shall be confounded.

SACRIFICIAL GIVING

When God sees a sacrificial offering, an offering that costs, He knows it. There are offerings, but some offerings provoke heaven to open and respond instantly. Sacrificial giving is one way to unlock doors in our lives and release God's blessings. Consider the examples below.

☑ *Offering of Abel*

This type of sacrificial giving gets the respect of heaven. God noticed the offering of Abel; it touched His heart. There are some breakthroughs a person will receive when there is a connection with God at this level.

GENESIS 4:3–5

And in process of time it came to pass, that Cain brought of the fruit of the ground an offering unto the LORD. And Abel, he also brought of the firstlings of his flock and of the fat thereof. And the LORD had respect unto Abel and to his offering: But unto Cain and to his offering he had not respect. And Cain was very wroth, and his countenance fell.

☑ *Offering of Noah*

This kind of offering connects a person's life to the covenant.

GENESIS 8:20–22

And Noah builded an altar unto the LORD; and took of every clean beast, and of every clean fowl, and offered burnt offerings on the altar. And the LORD smelled a sweet savour; and the LORD said in his heart, I will not again curse the ground any more for man's sake; for the imagination of man's heart is evil from his youth; neither will I again smite any more everything living, as I have done.

What brought this pronouncement was the offering of Noah. What the Lord smelled provoked what the Lord said. Abraham offered his Isaac to God, and it provoked God to release eternal covenant into his life. Friends, there are some doors you can provoke to open through sacrificial giving to God.

☑ *Offering of Solomon*

This type of sacrifice puts the resources of heaven at your disposal.

1 KINGS 3:3–5

And Solomon loved the LORD, walking in the statutes of David his father: only he sacrificed and burnt incense in high places. And the king went to **Gibeon** to sacrifice there; for that was the great high place: a thousand burnt offerings did Solomon offer upon that altar. In **Gibeon** the LORD appeared to Solomon in a dream by night: and God said, Ask what I shall give thee.

Gibeon was a place of a thousand (expensive) offerings. Solomon did something nobody before him had done. His unusual sacrifice caught God's attention, and the same night God appeared to him.

God appears spontaneously whenever you go to "Gibeon." There are certain revelations of God that cannot be received anywhere but in the "Gibeon" of sacrifice. You need to locate a "Gibeon" where you can sow a seed of life that will open your heaven perpetually. Sacrifice opened the door to an unlimited supply of wisdom, gold, and silver for Solomon. It unlocked and released God's best into his hands.

1 KINGS 3:13

And I have also given thee that which thou hast not asked, both riches, and honour: so that there shall not be any among the kings like unto thee all thy days.

MALACHI 3:10

Bring ye all the tithes into the storehouse, that there may be meat in mine house, and prove me now herewith, saith the LORD of hosts, if I will not open you **the windows** of heaven, and pour you out a blessing, that there shall not be room enough to receive it.

Heaven has "windows," and it seeks an outlet on earth where it can pour its abundant favor, grace, and provisions.

Chapter 6

THE STRUGGLE OF JACOB

"I WILL NOT LET YOU GO UNTIL..."

THE STRUGGLE OF JACOB
GENESIS 32:24–28

And Jacob was left alone; and there wrestled a man with
him until the breaking of the day. And when he saw that he
prevailed not against him, he touched the hollow of his thigh;
and the hollow of Jacob's thigh was out of joint, as he wrestled
with him. And he said, Let me go, for the day breaketh. And
he said, I will not let thee go, except thou bless me. And he
said unto him, What is thy name? And he said, Jacob. And he
said, Thy name shall be called no more Jacob, but Israel: for
as a prince hast thou power with God and with men, and hast
prevailed.

Some definite breakthrough will not come until we are left alone,
detached from men's promises and connections. Jacob fought and
persevered for his destiny, and even heaven recognized his persistence.
The fight for our destiny demands persistence and determination. "I
will not let thee go" was the cry of a man fighting for his life, his future, and his family. Many give up too soon in a fight, and they miss
their miracle.

Prayer is also called "travail" in the Bible. It is compared with a
woman who at the end of her pregnancy is due for delivery. As soon as
her water breaks, she is rushed into the labor room where she would
deliver a living being. Oftentimes the pain is intense and the hours
roll by slowly. She is sweating and in agony and constantly urged by
health workers to push, push, and push again. Unless she pushes,
the baby, though ready to come out, will not be able to do so. Then
suddenly, the pressure builds up until it reaches a peak with one final
push...and out the baby is born.

ISAIAH 66:7–8

Before she travailed, she brought forth; before her pain came,
she was delivered of a man child.
Who hath heard such a thing? who hath seen such things?
Shall the earth be made to bring forth in one day? or shall a nation be born at once? for as soon as Zion travailed, she brought
forth her children.

Prayer is often like that. Some dreams and desires are not ready to come forth until pressure is applied. Many dreams and ideas are miscarried at the point of delivery because the bearer fails to push when required. Some become weak, weary, and discouraged in the final lap of the journey; the opposition was too stiff and the resistance too strong. They simply gave up; their faith failed!

The size of the desired miracle will often determine the extent of the struggle. Daniel's prayer was resisted for twenty-one days because of its implications in the world. A principality was dispatched by the devil to obstruct the answer. There was war and confrontation in the spiritual realm because Daniel refused to let go. He was not ready to give up in defeat. He continued to push harder with each passing day. His persistence sustained him and fueled the battle until the angel Michael showed up.

When you are not seeing results, it is not an indication that your prayers are not reaching God. It is the right moment to push and knock harder and louder.

PRAY UNTIL SOMETHING HAPPENS (PUSH)

Don't surrender to defeat and give up when you are knocking the door of heaven over a difficult situation. Sometimes heaven appears to be silent: no word, no revelation, no direction. Everything seems to be at a standstill. Then you begin to think your effort is futile. Keep on praying, Jesus inferred in John 16:24, until your joy is full. In other words, He was saying to keep pushing until something happens.

THE FOUNDATION OF LIFE

PSALM 11:3
If the foundations be destroyed, what can the righteous do?

The foundation of many people is the source of their woes. If it is destroyed, nothing else built on it can be successful. For Jacob his foundation was faulty. Right from birth, something went wrong. He got a wrong name because of the circumstances around his birth. He held on to the heel of his brother, Esau, and they gave him his name,

"Jacob," meaning a supplanter or a cheat (see Genesis 25:26). This was not the name heaven designed for him. His name was wrong, his foundation was faulty, and it affected his character in life. He eventually cheated his brother of his birthright, true to his name. Esau lamented that Jacob lived up to his name: "Is he not rightly named Jacob? For he has supplanted me these two times. He took away my birthright; and behold, now he has taken away my blessing" (Genesis 27:36).

Everywhere Jacob went, nothing worked. His entire life was a catalogue of struggles and disappointment. His father-in-law cheated him in marriage, switched his wife Rachel, ten times his wages was changed. He became very frustrated, and little wonder why he was desperate when he met the angel. Something had to change.

You may need to examine the foundation of your life, dear friend; something in your past might be the reason for your troubles. Is your name working against you? Your family background or your family history may give some clues to the source of the problem you face today. Thanks to God, who has given us victory through the blood of Jesus to deal with such things.

The one thing the angel changed in Jacob was his name. "What is your name?" he asked. "Jacob" he replied. And he said, "Thy name shall be called no more Jacob, but Israel: for as a prince hast thou power with God and with men, and hast prevailed." The wrong foundation was broken through the name change. He got a new "social security" from God; the covenant he was to carry alongside Abraham and Isaac could not be built on a faulty ground!

NAME CHANGE

Jacob was not the only person whose name God changed in the Scriptures. The Lord did the same for others; He changed Abram to Abraham; Sarai to Sarah; Saul became Paul; and Simon the unstable became *Cephas*, or Peter the Rock. God does so to reflect the promise and His plans for an individual. The greatest name change a person must experience for God's blessings to flow is to be called a "son" of God. This happens at conversion. As many as receive Jesus, He gave them power to become sons of God (see John 1:12).

QUIT STRUGGLING, START TRUSTING

God wants to free your life from struggling. In Christ, we are too blessed to be stressed. Unfortunately, many believers live a life of struggle; like Jacob, we think everything depends on our efforts, our skills, and how smart we are. There is enough grace in God to break the cycle of struggle and frustration in our lives.

Meaning of Struggle

1. To contend with an adversary or opposing force. Your life journey is difficult because of the forces opposing you.
2. To advance with violent effort, as if there is a ceiling and limitation over your life.
3. A war, fight, conflict, or contest of any kind. Every accomplishment is like a fight; some people have been fighting since infancy.

For some the struggle takes place in their career, others in their marriage. Some are struggling financially, while for others life is just tough and slow. Many things don't work.

- What are indications that we are struggling?
- When input does not match output. When you work so much and get so little.
- When you go around in circles, feeling frustrated and stagnated.
- When things that don't require much effort take so much sweating. You constantly have mountains bigger than you.

Why Do People Struggle?

1. Sin and disobedience

This can be clearly seen in Adam after the Fall. This was the origin of struggle in the life of man. Sin will bring chaos and disorderliness into the plans of God for a man. Until sin came, Adam and Eve knew no lack. Work was a pleasure, not a burden. They had peace with themselves and all the elements around them. Animals respected them until disobedience came, then the dog barked at them, snakes would bite them, and the lion would tear them apart. The glory was gone from their lives, along with the honor that glory brings with it.

Afterward, the curse was released over man's work; the land was cursed for him. Sin will affect the work of your hands and your productivity. Man must labor more to get fruitfulness because the land is hard.

We also see the consequences of disobedience when Jonah ran away from God:

Jonah 1:3

But Jonah rose up to flee unto Tarshish from the presence of the LORD, and **went down to** Joppa; and he found a ship going to Tarshish: so he paid the fare thereof, **and went down into** it, to go with them unto Tarshish from the presence of the LORD.

Disobedience takes you away from God's presence and opens you to demonic assaults and dangers. When Jonah turned his back in disobedience, everything began to go downhill for him. The day a man begins to disobey God, the downward trend begins in his life. Find out why things are going down around you and in your family. There may be "strange stuff" in your boat.

2. Power of a curse working against one's life

a. Adam

Genesis 3:17–19

And unto Adam he said, Because thou hast hearkened unto the voice of thy wife, and hast eaten of the tree, of which I commanded thee, saying, Thou shalt not eat of it: cursed is the ground for thy sake; *in sorrow shalt thou eat of it all the days of thy life:*
Thorns also and thistles shall it bring forth to thee; and thou shalt eat the herb of the field;

In the sweat of thy face shalt thou eat bread, till thou return unto the ground; for out of it was thou taken: for dust thou art, and unto dust shalt thou return.

b. Cain

GENESIS 4:10–13

And he said, What hast thou done? the voice of thy brother's blood crieth unto me from the ground.
And now art thou cursed from the earth, which hath opened her mouth to receive thy brother's blood from thy hand;
When thou tillest the ground, it shall not henceforth yield unto thee her strength; a fugitive and a vagabond shalt thou be in the earth.
And Cain said unto the LORD, My punishment is greater than I can bear.

3. Law of Sowing and Reaping

The law of sowing and reaping will always catch up with a man. Jacob had cheated others; he, too, was cheated. He stole a birthright, his wife was stolen; he deceived his father with a cloth, and his sons deceived him with a cloth.

The reason you are struggling in some areas of your life may be Nemesis catching up with you. Go and settle some things in your past and your future will be released.

4. Ignorance

Lack of knowledge is a major factor why many people struggle in life. Paul prayed for our eyes of understanding to be enlightened that we may comprehend the provisions of heaven at our disposal.

5. Lack of Wisdom

Wisdom is better than strength, says God's Word. When wisdom is lacking, struggle is inevitable. Wisdom is to know what to do at critical junctions of life. It is the application of knowledge. The struggle many have in marriage and business is not a lack of money, but a lack of wisdom to manage what they have.

Ecclesiastes 9:16–18

Then said I, Wisdom is better than strength… Wisdom is better than weapons of war…

For our lives to be struggle-free, we need to realize that

1. **Nothing can be received or added except from the Lord.**

John 3:27

John answered and said, A man can receive nothing, except it be given him from heaven.

Whatever door the Lord has not opened for you, you will break it if you force yourself to open it. When the Lord is not there, failure is imminent and inevitable. Many are struggling with a lot of things in their lives because it was not the Lord that initiated them. He is Alpha and Omega; He cannot be the Omega where he was not the Alpha.

If God did not give it, don't get it at all cost, or it will cost your soul. When He gives it to you, you get it. If He did not, if you get it, it will bring you trouble.

We must not behave like Jacob, who thought the way to be blessed was to scheme his brother out of his birthright. Such behavior can turn you into a crook, a cheat, and a liar.

2. **A life of trust in the Lord will free us from struggling**

When we don't trust God, we trust other things: horses/chariots, men, materials, social security, government, etc.

Psalm 20:7

Some trust in chariots, and some in horses: but we will remember the name of the LORD our God.

Psalm 146:3–5

Put not your trust in princes, nor in the son of man, in whom there is no help. His breath goeth forth, he returneth to his earth; in that very day his thoughts perish. Happy is he that hath the God of Jacob for his help, whose hope is in the LORD his God:

We fail to recognize Him as our source. We think our sustenance comes from our ability and struggle. It is the covenant that feeds us, not our big salaries. We believe with our heads, but our hearts refuse to trust Him; we divide our eggs into different baskets just in case He fails, and we have devised other alternatives in case the Lord does not come through.

We are failing because of the things we lean on. Whatever we trust will fail us eventually if it is not God. Trust and obey, there is no other way. You are not happy because you don't trust Him. The extent of your joy is determined by the level of your trust.

I remember a funny story of an old man. To celebrate his seventy-fifth birthday, an aviation enthusiast offered to take him for a plane ride over the little West Virginia town where he had spent all his life. The old man accepted the offer. Back on the ground, after circling over the town twenty minutes, his friend asked, "Were you scared, Uncle Dudley?" "No-o-o," was the hesitant answer. "But I never did put my full weight down."

Jesus is strong enough to bear us on His shoulders, so put your weight down.

Chapter 7

LET GO, LET GOD!

A young man who was struggling to let the Lord have His way in his life knelt to pray. He had been advised to "let God do the work for him." But as he was kneeling, he cried, "I want to let God have His way, but I can't."

The day before he had cut out of pasteboard the letters "LET GOD" and tacked them on the wall. He rose from his knees and with a feeling of defeat and despair, he left the room and slammed the door with a bang, saying, "I can't LET GOD."

On his return to his room, he was startled to note that the slam of the door had loosened the letter D on the word GOD, causing it to fall to the floor, and changing the motto to "LET GO."

"I will, I will, Lord Jesus," he cried and threw himself on his knees at the side of his bed. "I will let go, and let God," and he did. —Gospel for the Youth

Prayer is meant to free us from the worry and anxiety of life; however, many people pray and still worry. They pray with one eye closed and the other one roaming around for an alternative solution, or what many call Plan B. This is an indication we are not fully trusting God in the matter of our lives and not fully releasing our burdens into His able hands.

Such an attitude displeases God, and it is the very reason why many prayers are not answered. If we give God our battles and surrender to Him as our commanding officer, we are only expected to follow Him and not order Him around or dictate how the battle should be fought. There must be a place of surrender in our prayer...when we completely leave the outcome to God. When we do that, we become free of stress and we can sleep well at night.

Jesus slept through the storm while His disciples were running helter-skelter. He knew who He was and the care of the Father for Him. The noise of the waves did not bother Him; He was peaceful and calm while others went through the torture and tension of an imminent death. Can you sleep when your house is seemingly on fire?

Isaiah 26:3

Thou wilt keep him in perfect peace, whose mind is stayed on thee: because he trusteth in thee.

This is a powerful promise for those who will let go and let God handle their problems. Many of us cannot sit still in our battles; we feel must be doing something and in the process we begin to do the wrong thing. We have not learned the meaning of the instruction God gave to Jehoshaphat when he was confronted by a large army:

2 Chronicles 20:17

> *The more we pray, the less we worry; the more we worry the less we pray. Why worry when you can pray?*

Ye shall not need to fight in this battle: set yourselves, stand ye still, and see the salvation of the Lord with you, O Judah and Jerusalem: fear not, nor be dismayed; to morrow go out against them: for the Lord will be with you.

In Psalm 46:10 we are admonished to "be still, and know that I am God: I will be exalted among the heathen, I will be exalted in the earth." When you find yourself not remaining still and free from sleeplessness, fear, and anxiety, it is an indication you have not let go.

A woman once traveling on a ship was caught up in a violent storm. Everyone was rushing around to lighten the ship and struggling to prevent the ship from going down. All hands were "on deck," except for this Christian lady. She just went to her cabin to sleep. While in this mess, someone caught the attention she was not involved in the running around, to which she confidently replied, "Why do I need to stay awake when my Captain, the Lord Jesus, is in control of the ship?"

Jesus, the Captain of our salvation, is very competent and highly experienced. He is referred to as "a man of war." The apostle Paul confidently declared that He is able to handle what is committed to His hands; what He began, He will finish.

PHILIPPIANS 1:6
Being confident of this very thing, that he which hath begun a
good work in you will perform it until the day of Jesus Christ.

Let go of your worries, your fear, and your panic, and enjoy the
perfect peace that comes with prayer. In your desperate moment,
remember He still in control. He never leaves His throne or loses His
grip on the universe He created.

FROM PRISON TO PRAISE
After all is said and done, you must turn your praise on. The most
dangerous time to praise God is when nothing else makes sense, when
the enemy expects weeping from your mouth and tears from your
eyes, then you suddenly burst into songs of praise. This is what I call
"radical praise."

Radical praise will produce a revolution to all ugly situations of
life whenever it is practiced on a consistent basis. When the situation
looks desperate, try radical praise—sacrificial praise!

Are you in some trouble where there seems to be no way out? Are
you in some midnight crisis when all help has failed? When it seems
your dreams are dying and you are on a tightrope…try radical praise!

Worship, praise, and thanksgiving in the darkest hour of your life
will repel the thickest of darkness in your soul. When pain and troubles
circle us all around, we must give them back to God in worship.

JOB 1:20–21
Then Job arose, and rent his mantle, and shaved his head, and
fell down upon the ground, and worshipped,

A DIFFICULT CIRCUMSTANCE (ACTS 16:16–24)
It was an ugly night for Paul and Silas. The devil was very angry
and raised his battalion against them. Hell broke loose; the demons
were running wild. God's servants were beaten and bleeding, and
everything had gone bad. To the surprise of hell, God's servants were
cool and calm. They had everything under the control of praise.

The devil was really angry, the magistrates went crazy, and the jailor placed them with bad criminals. Yet they were in the center of God's will, and that was the reason the devil was mad!

A STRANGE AND SURPRISING RESPONSE

ACTS 16:25

And at midnight Paul and Silas prayed, and sang praises unto God: and the prisoners heard them.

Negative situations in life provide God with an opportunity to be glorified. You may be bound physically, but never let the devil bind your mouth, your praise. The problem of your problem is what you do with the problem. It either breaks you down or gives you a break-through. You can either cry or smile.

What do men naturally do?

Some men break down at bad situations, while others break forth and break through out of drought and dryness with singing and praises. Some run around seeking help and sympathy, and some folks will pray a little casual prayer, asking "why" repeatedly, accuse God of mismanaging their lives, blame other people for their woes, grumble, and complain.

Dr. David Soper, in *God Is Inescapable*, suggests that basically the difference between a prison and a monastery is just the difference between griping and gratitude. Undoubtedly this is true. Imprisoned criminals spend every waking moment griping; "self-imprisoned" saints spend every waking moment offering thanks. Dr. Soper says that when a criminal becomes a saint, a prison may become a monastery; when a saint gives up gratitude, a monastery may become a prison.

What did Paul and Silas not do?

- They had no regret, no retreat, no apology to the devil, and no self-pity. They were not sorry for serving and obeying God. They reached a point of no return in their commitment and were willing to lay down their lives if required.

- They did not blame God or each other. They knew that God is good at all times even if they could not figure out what was going on or what God was doing about the situation.
- They refused to allow the circumstance to weigh them down. They were in good spirits. Whatever the devil touches in your life, don't let him touch your joy.

WHAT TO DO IN THE DARKEST HOURS OF OUR LIVES

1. Count your many blessings, one by one.
2. Focus on God's goodness, rather than the devil's wickedness.
3. Make a choice: sacrifice of praise. Rejoice.

Whatever stops your joy steals your strength. Satan wants to steal it by giving you reasons to cry, wallow in self-pity, and pull up the comparison chart with your friends and neighbors. Praise is the way for victory over fear.

Do you know what praise does in times of trouble and desperation? God and the angels are "surprised"—pleasantly surprised that you choose praise instead of complaint. The devil and his cohorts are "shocked"—grievously shocked and disappointed that you ignore their taunting. Your friend and enemies are "stunned"—unbelievably stunned to see you rejoicing when they expect you to be grumpy and down.

H. G. Bosch gave a beautiful illustration of a man singing in a wheelchair. It goes like this:

While walking along a busy street one day, I heard someone singing. His sweet voice was distinguishable even above the noise of the traffic. When I located him, I noticed that he had no legs and was pushing himself through the crowd in a wheelchair.

Catching up with him, I said, "I want you to know, friend, that to hear singing from a person in your condition gives everyone else a lift."

He answered with a grateful smile, "When I stopped looking at what I had lost and began concentrating on all I had left, I found much for which I could rejoice and be happy."

PSALM 22:3
But thou art holy, O thou that inhabitest the praises of Israel.

ACTS 16:26
And suddenly there was a great earthquake, so that the foundations of the prison were shaken: and immediately all the doors were opened, and every one's bands were loosed.

Suddenly God's presence showed up inside the prison. He did not send an angel like the time of Peter in prison; instead His very presence filled the jailhouse. The doors flung open, the iron chains were broken, and the prisoners were loosed. The praise of God has done it again. Praise can transport you from your current prison into freedom.

When confusion shows up, release God's presence through praise. No devil can match God's presence.

Conclusion

100 PRAYER POINTS FOR DIFFERENT DESPERATE SITUATIONS

A. FIGHTING IN DESPERATE FINANCIAL SITUATIONS

1. Rebuke every devourer around your finances.
2. Declare unusual, uncommon doors of provision and supplies.
3. Break the cycle of lack and poverty over your life and family.
4. Praise God and prophesy the anointing for fruitfulness and blessings into your life.
5. Declare the removal of all spirit of limitations over your life. Demand the removal of the hands of the enemy from your finances.
6. Pray for the miracle of debt cancellation.
7. Ask the Lord by faith for a season of financial rest and termination of struggle.
8. Ask the Lord for a heart of giving and become a faithful steward of resources.
9. Declare that you will be a lender not a borrower, a giver not a beggar.
10. Give thanks for releasing into your life the power to make wealth.

B. FIGHTING FOR YOUR FAMILY AND CHILDREN

11. Bring your family under the cover of the blood of Jesus.
12. Destroy every curse and hold of the wicked over your family.
13. Deliver your children from the spirit of rebellion and shield them from a wayward spirit.
14. Cancel every plan of evil and premature death over your loved ones.
15. Prophesy favor, grace, success, and breakthrough into your family life and over your children.
16. Declare salvation over your household, and the transformation of the lives of unsaved loved ones.
17. Place a demand over the future of your family and declare greatness over your children.
18. Speak peace, love, joy, wisdom, and grace into your household.
19. Arrest the spirit of confusion, strife, and misunderstanding over your family.
20. Decree good health and long life in your family.

C. FIGHTING FOR YOUR MARRIAGE

21. Draw the blood line against the spirit of divorce in your marriage.
22. Nullify the arrows of wickedness, division, and confusion in your marriage.
23. Break negative tendencies, spells, and pronouncements contrary to your marriage.
24. Establish peace and joy in your home.
25. Ask God to pour the fresh wine of love into your marriage.
26. Pray that your marriage will honor the Lord and bring praise to His name.
27. Thank God that His banner over your marriage is love.
28. Speak healing and restoration to your marriage. Peace and harmony will reign.
29. Pray for your spouse's health, work, mind, emotions, protection, and provision.
30. Close the door to your home against every intruder and contrary force trying to invade your marriage.

D. FIGHTING AGAINST DESPERATE HEALTH PROBLEMS, SICK-NESS, OR DANGER OF DEATH

31. Demand that the enemy remove his hands from your health.
32. Praise God, for by His stripes you were healed.
33. Declare that you will not die but live to testify to God's goodness.
34. From the crown of your head to the soles of your feet, uproot whatever God has not planted.
35. Pronounce that the Spirit of God that dwells in you shall quicken your mortal body.
36. Reject every negative report of sickness and disease; release the report of the Lord that says you are healed.
37. Receive the manifestation of the covenant of His peace and healing.
38. Cut off the rod of the wicked over your life, remove the spirit of affliction, and demand its departure.
39. Pray that the Lord will add years to your life as He did for Hezekiah.
40. Thank God for the manifestation of your healing.

E. FIGHTING SPIRITUAL AND DEMONIC ATTACKS

41. Take your stand in faith and victory and declare you are a victor over the forces of darkness.
42. Release God's Word, that no weapon fashioned against you shall prosper; condemn every tongue that rises up against you.
43. Declare as null and void every enchantment and evil pronouncement against your life.
44. Return every arrow to its sender. Root out every device planted against your well-being.
45. Speak boldly that greater is He that is in you than he that is against you.
46. Pray to lift the standard of the Spirit against the flood of wickedness trying to overtake you.
47. Overthrow the dominion of the kingdom of darkness over your life; establish the Kingdom of righteousness.

48. Pronounce your victory spiritually, emotionally, and physically over every battles in the heavenlies.
49. Pull down every stronghold of wickedness in your life.
50. Thank God that He makes you to triumph in Christ and that you are more than a conqueror.

F. FIGHTING FAILURE AND LACK OF PROGRESS
51. Thank God for the promise He has spoken concerning your life, that you will be the head and not the tail.
52. Speak against the forces of frustration working against your progress and success in life. Destroy every chain slowing down your advancement.
53. Dismantle every spiritual opposition arrayed against the purpose of God for your blessing in life.
54. Ask the Lord for speed and acceleration in your life to catch up with lost years and opportunities, like He did for Elijah when he outran Ahab.
55. Pray against the spirit of discouragement and despair pulling you to give up.
56. Ask the Lord to open before you doors of opportunities and to do something new in your life.
57. Pray for divine connection to helpers of your destiny wherever they may be.
58. Declare that the Lord will restore to you what the cankerworm and locusts have eaten out of your life.
59. Pray that the failure you face will become an opportunity for outstanding success.
60. Declare that you are not a failure; you are blessed, successful, and highly favored.

G. FIGHTING THE ENEMY
61. Ask the Lord to expose every enemy troubling your life and your family.
62. Ask the Lord to take over the battles of your life and fight for you.

63. Soak yourself, your family, and your future in the blood of Jesus. You will be inaccessible to the enemy.

64. Ask the Lord to teach your hands to fight and your fingers to war.

65. Declare your victory in Christ Jesus; declare that you are more than a conqueror through His power that works in you.

66. Pull down every Goliath in your life in the name of the Lord, ask the Lord to disgrace the giants intimidating you.

67. Ask the Lord to give you a spirit of boldness and courage to face every enemy in battle. Root out the spirit of fear and intimidation.

68. Declare complete rest in every aspect of your life, your warfare to be accomplished, and the storm to be over.

69. Thank God because He is your "Jehovah Nissi," the Captain of your life and the "Man of War" fighting for you.

70. Declare victory in Jesus' name.

H. FIGHTING WHEN FACING DANGERS AND TROUBLES

71. Declare, "I am marked as untouchable. Let no man, demons, or whoever trouble me" (Galatians 6:17).

72. Raise the standard of the blood against impending dangers and troubles over your household. Draw the blood line over your property.

73. Frustrate the plans and tokens of the enemy against your life. Take a stand against every demonic aggression in the name of the Lord.

74. Pull a wall of defense and shield of protection over your life and family from the arrows of the wicked.

75. Declare over your life that the siege of the enemy be broken and the trap of the wicked be destroyed.

76. Confess and declare Psalm 27:5 over your life: "For in the time of trouble he shall hide me in his pavilion: in the secret of his tabernacle shall he hide me; he shall set me up upon a rock."

77. Declare Job 5:19 over your life and family: "He shall deliver thee in six troubles: yea, in seven there shall no evil touch thee."

78. Ask the Lord to fight your battles for you as the Captain of the Host of your army.
79. Pray that the Lord will overturn the table of the wicked and give you a testimony out of the desperate situation.
80. Confess Isaiah 50:7: "For the Lord GOD will help me; therefore shall I not be confounded: therefore have I set my face like a flint, and I know that I shall not be ashamed."
81. Declare that you will never be ashamed in life; you will not be confounded (Isaiah 30:15).

J. FIGHTING WHEN YOU DON'T KNOW WHAT TO DO NEXT

82. Ask the Lord to open the eyes of your understanding to His plans for your life.
83. Pray that the Holy Spirit will direct your path and order your footsteps.
84. Eliminate every confusion in your mind, ask God to shine His light on your life.
85. Pray for divine intervention in every area of your life.
86. Release helpers of destiny to your path. Pray for divine connection with the right people.
87. Ask God that every blessing and miracle that has your name on it will locate you.
88. Pray that you will be at the right place, at the right time, and with the right people who will connect you to your miracle.
89. Pray for strength and grace to confront every obstacle on your path.
90. Ask God to make a way for you out of your current situation (Isaiah 43:19).

K. FIGHTING WHEN LIFE KNOCKS YOU DOWN

91. Pray for God's mighty deliverance from your present predicament.
92. Ask God to turn the situation around for you by His mighty hands.
93. Speak to your mountain to bow in the name of the Lord (Zechariah 4:7).

94. Pray that your head will be unbowed and your spirit remain intact in whatever situation you are facing.
95. Declare that the joy of the Lord is your strength and that the enemy cannot steal your joy.
96. Pray for restoration and recovery of everything that the enemy has stolen from your life. Declare, "I will pursue, overtake, and recover" whatever you have lost in time, opportunities, and resources.
97. Speak a new beginning and a fresh start in every area of your life. Declare the dawn of a new season over the work of your hands.
98. Ask God to make your feet like hinds' feet and set you up on high places (Psalm 18:33).
99. Give thanks to God because He is the God of second chances
100. Thank Him for His faithfulness, mercy, and wisdom over your life.

BIBLIOGRAPHY

1. Butler, John G., *Daily Bible Reading*, Sermonettes #1 (Clinton, Iowa: LBC Publications, 2004).
2. Higle, Tommy C., *Journey into Blessed Living, A Study of the Beatitudes* (Marietta, OK: Tommy Hingle Publishers, 2009).
3. Soper, David Wesley, *God Is Inescapable* (Philadelphia, PA: Westminster Press, 1959).
4. Tan, Dr. Paul Lee, *Encyclopedia of 15,000 Illustrations,* "Signs of the Times" (Dallas, Texas: Bible Communications Inc, 1998).).

To order additional copies of

DESPERATE PRAYERS FOR DESPERATE SITUATIONS

have your credit card ready and call
From USA: (800) 917-BOOK (2665)
From Canada: (877) 855-6732

or e-mail
orders@selahbooks.com

or order online at
www.selahbooks.com

CPSIA information can be obtained at www.ICGtesting.com
Printed in the USA
LVOW071747020413

327242LV00025B/1121/P